Concentrate

Free o...
and revisio...

C000003656

Visit the online resource centre at:

www.oup.com/lawrevision/

Take your learning further:

➤ Multiple-choice questions

➤ An interactive glossary

➤ Outline exam answers

➤ Flashcards of key cases

➤ Download our free ebook, *Study and Exam Success for Law Students,* which includes:

• Guidance on how to approach revision and prepare for exams

• Guidance on how to use a statute book

'I always buy a Concentrate revision guide for each module and use the online resources. The **outline answers are particularly helpful** and I often use **the multiple-choice questions to test my basic understanding** of a topic'

Alice Reilly,
Cardiff University

'The Online Resource Centre has been **exceptionally useful.** In my first year, I used the resources to **quiz myself,** to **test my knowledge and understanding of cases,** and **to pick up extra pointers that could give me a few extra marks**'

Kelly Newman, University
of Exeter

consolidate knowledge > focus revision > maximise potential

To my students, whose questions and answers (right and wrong) provided the inspiration for this book

Intellectual Property
Concentrate

3rd Edition

Tim Press

Lecturer in Law, Cardiff University

OXFORD
UNIVERSITY PRESS

Great Clarendon Street, Oxford, OX2 6DP,
United Kingdom

Oxford University Press is a department of the University of Oxford.
It furthers the University's objective of excellence in research, scholarship,
and education by publishing worldwide. Oxford is a registered trade mark of
Oxford University Press in the UK and in certain other countries

First edition 2013
Second edition 2015
Impression: 1

Public sector information reproduced under Open Government Licence v3.0
(http://www.nationalarchives.gov.uk/doc/open-government-licence/open-government-licence.htm)

Published in the United States of America by Oxford University Press
198 Madison Avenue, New York, NY 10016, United States of America

British Library Cataloguing in Publication Data
Data available

Library of Congress Control Number: 2017933304

ISBN 978–0–19–880388–1

Printed in Great Britain by
Bell & Bain Ltd., Glasgow

New to this edition

- The impact of Brexit on IP law is briefly summarized, in general and in relation to specific issues.

- The key changes introduced by the amended Trade Mark Regulation are noted and discussed.

- Important case-law developments in relation to communication to the public, infringement of copyright in entrepreneurial works, and the need for UK-based goodwill in actions for passing-off are included.

Contents

Table of cases

Table of cases
✱✱✱✱✱✱✱✱✱✱✱✱

Table of cases

✳✳✳✳✳✳✳✳✳✳✳

Table of legislation

Table of legislation

✶✶✶✶✶✶✶✶✶✶✶✶

Table of legislation
✽✽✽✽✽✽✽✽✽✽✽✽

#1

Introduction to intellectual property and common themes

The different rights that fall under the heading 'intellectual property' (IP) are given in the list that follows. In this regard, there is a reasonable amount of international agreement on what types of legal right are part of IP law.

- The protection of original **works** by copyright and of the author's personal relationship to the work by moral rights.

- The protection of sound recordings and other 'fixations' of works by **neighbouring rights** and for performers by performers' rights (and database right in the EU).

- The protection of secret information (and personal privacy in the UK, although in many jurisdictions that would be regarded as quite separate).

- The protection of inventions by patents (and in some jurisdictions, although not the UK, utility models or design patents).

- *The protection of plant varieties by plant breeders' rights.*

- The protection of product design by registered designs, copyright, and other rights (in the UK by design right and in the EU by registered designs).

- *The protection of semiconductor topographies.*

- The protection of brands by registered trade marks, and various legal measures to protect traders against misleading and unfair competitive behaviour (in the UK, the law of passing-off, in other jurisdictions laws of unfair trading).

- *The protection of geographical indications and names associated with a locality.*

Introduction

This book focuses on the rights as they apply in the UK, including rights created by the EU, such as database right. The rights in italics are not covered.

Legal systems around the world have seen fit to create these rights or causes of action to protect intangible concepts such as inventions, literature, brands, designs, and so on. It is said that IP protects the products of the mind, but that does not really apply to brand protection or to the protection of some types of information.

The main UK rights and their legal bases are set out in Table 1.1.

Table 1.1 Intellectual property rights and their legal bases

Registered rights	Automatic rights	Main statutes	Main treaties
Patents (UK and European)		Patents Act 1977	– TRIPs (substantive law) – European Patent Convention (substantive) – Paris Convention (recognition and priority) – Patent Co-Operation Treaty (international applications)
Registered designs (UK)		Registered Designs Act 1949 Directive 98/71	– TRIPs (substantive law) – Paris Convention (recognition and priority)
Registered designs (EU)		Regulation 6/2002	As above
	EU unregistered right	Regulation 6/2002	None
	Design right ('UK unregistered design right')	Copyright Designs and Patents Act 1988	None
Trade marks (UK)		Trade Marks Act 1994 Directive 2008/95	– TRIPs (substantive law) – Paris Convention (recognition and priority) – Madrid Agreement (international applications)
Trade marks (EU)		Regulation 2015/2424	As above

Copyright, moral rights, and performers' rights	Copyright, Designs and Patents Act 1988 Numerous Directives	Literary, dramatic, artistic, or musical works and moral rights: – Berne Convention – WIPO Copyright Treaty Sound recordings and performers' rights: – Rome Convention – WIPO Performances and Phonograms Treaty
Database right	Copyright and Rights in Databases Regulations 1997	None
Non-statutory rights		
Passing-off		None
Trade secrets and personal privacy		TRIPs (trade secrets)

Theory and intellectual property

As IP rights are so diverse, the theoretical bases for legal protection vary and are dealt with separately in their relevant chapters. However, there are some common approaches.

Neo-classical micro-economic theory

This branch of economics looks at the behaviour of individual players in a market and assumes they will try to make rational decisions about what to buy and (if they are in business) what products or services to offer and at what price. It therefore only applies to market economies. The content of IP rights is information, and once a work, invention, or product has been made available, that information is often made public and can be easily shared. Economists say such things are 'common goods', meaning that everyone (not only the person who originally created, purchased, or commissioned the work) can share the benefits. This is in contrast to other goods, such as a bicycle, which can only be ridden by one person at a time and which cannot be copied without incurring the same costs of production as the original maker.

There is a problem when one tries to apply a market model to the production of common goods: there is no incentive to invest in, for example, creating a new musical work and sharing it with an audience because once the work is public there is no mechanism for the author to continue to extract revenue from the use of the work.

Economic theory recognizes that in these situations, if there is a public benefit from the production of the common goods, some form of intervention is needed in the market in order to ensure that they are produced. In the case of IP, this intervention is in the form of laws creating legal property rights, which give creators and inventors something to sell in the marketplace flowing from their intellectual efforts.

The concept of there being a benefit from the production of the subject matter of the right is important. The legal intervention is only needed if, and to the extent that, it encourages the production of things that the public values (new films, shiny new gadgets, etc). The corollary of this is that a legal intervention that results in no increase in the production of such goods, or which has negative side effects, should not be made. Examples of negative effects are restrictions on freedom of expression or on the production of derivative works or inventions. Thus, economic theory indicates that IP rights should exist, but their scope, duration, and effects should be carefully judged. Having too much IP can be as bad as having too little.

In more general terms, economists recognize that wherever there is 'market failure', a legal intervention is needed. Market failure can arise not only in the case of common goods but where other things, such as a lack of information or high transaction costs, get in the way of market operation. Lack of information is a basis for trade mark law, and transaction cost is one reason for allowing minor defences and exceptions to IP rights.

Rights-based and other approaches

Economic arguments are not the only reasons commonly used to justify IP. In many cases we recognize that the individual author, inventor, or businessman has natural rights to protect their work, invention, or brand, not because of economic theory, but because of our conceptions of rights and fairness. It is difficult to find the hard numbers to plug into the economists' equations, so very often IP law and policy is informed by these other considerations.

Common legal topics

These topics are dealt with here as they affect more than one IP right. Particular issues flowing from them will be mentioned in the following chapters.

International harmonization

An overview of the IP treaties

Apart from trade secrets and the protection of personal privacy, all areas of IP law are covered by specific international conventions. In addition, the **Agreement on Trade-Related Aspects of Intellectual Property** (**TRIPs** for short), which is part of the **General Agreement on Tariffs and Trade** (**GATT**), deals with all IP rights, including trade secrets, often by requiring compliance with an existing treaty (eg the **Berne Convention**).

Conventions can operate to harmonize national laws or, in the case of the registered rights, to provide for recognition of the priority of national applications and procedures for applying in many jurisdictions.

The treaties are discussed under the individual chapters. Table 1.1 lists the main ones applying to each right.

The legal effects of treaties

UK law does not recognize the legally binding effects of international treaties in domestic law. If domestic legislation implementing a treaty has not been passed, it has no legal effect. Where such a law has been passed, the precise terms of the treaty *may* be relevant to the process of statutory interpretation. This does not follow automatically; the intention of Parliament must be found, if necessary by looking at the parliamentary debates (following *Pepper v Hart* [1992]). There is an example of this in Chapter 4 ('Moral rights') in the *Pasterfield* [1999] case.

The previous paragraph does not apply to the EU treaties, treaties entered into at EU level, and EU legislation, where EU law principles apply.

EU harmonization

The laws of registered trade marks and registered designs have been fully codified by EU legislation, which has created EU-wide registered rights. Several aspects of copyright law, and one aspect of patent law, have been harmonized by means of EU Directives. In addition, the **Database Directive (96/9/EC)** created a whole new IP right, database right.

EU harmonizing Directives are incorporated into UK law by statutory instruments made under the **European Communities Act 1972**. In most cases, these operate to amend the provisions of the main act (the **Copyright Designs and Patents Act 1988** in the case of copyright, and so on). In cases where the provisions of the Directive do not fit within the scope of the main Act, the statutory instrument implements the law directly—this is the case with database right. An exception is trade marks, where in 1994 the **Trade Marks Act** was passed to implement the **Trade Marks Directive (89/104/EEC)**.

Wherever UK legislation is passed to implement EU law, the EU law doctrines of direct and indirect effects must be borne in mind. As Directives and Regulations are EU laws, legal issues may (and sometimes must) be referred by national courts to the European Court of Justice (ECJ) under the preliminary ruling procedure. The ECJ has ruled that national laws must be interpreted to be consistent with EU Directives, and that this can involve ignoring inconsistent national law provisions completely or applying a provision of a Directive even where it has not been implemented. UK courts recognize this and will interpret national law accordingly.

There are a few situations where the wording of the Act differs in a significant way from that of the Directive, or the Directive has been interpreted so that a false impression of the law could be given by reading the Act alone. These cases are highlighted in the relevant chapters.

Common legal topics
∗∗∗∗∗∗∗∗∗∗∗

The EU registered rights (trade marks and designs)

The legal structure of these registered rights is complex because:

- national laws have been harmonized by an EU Directive;
- applications can be made to national registration offices for national registered rights;
- an EU Regulation has set up an EU-wide registered right, which can be applied for to the EU Intellectual Property Office (EUIPO) in Alicante, Spain.

The substantive law governing the EU rights (in the Regulations) is the same as the harmonized law of the Directives; therefore, in practice you only need to learn one set of rules! There are differences of procedure between the two, but these are beyond the scope of this book.

This structure is summarized in Figure 1.1.

Appeals from the EUIPO go to the General Court (formerly the Court of First Instance), with a further appeal on points of law to the ECJ.

Brexit implications for intellectual property

The fate of the EU-wide registered rights in the UK (trade marks and designs granted by the EUIPO) will need to be clarified in the leaving arrangements. The Regulations

Figure 1.1 Structure of law governing EU rights

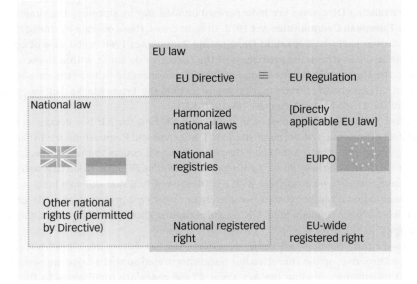

requiring these to be respected in the UK will cease to have effect in the absence of any agreement. The obvious solution to this is for the UK to recognize such registrations as UK registered rights. The leaving arrangements will also need to deal with the fate of applications in progress at the leaving date. Unless the UK arranges to continue to be part of these schemes, after leaving rights granted by the EUIPO will not cover the UK. By contrast, those aspects of EU law implemented by Directives will continue in force so long as the UK law implementing the Directive does. The difference in these cases will be that the UK courts will no longer be bound to follow the doctrine of the ECJ in areas where it has ruled on the interpretation of the underlying Directive. This will be a novel problem for the common law: will cases decided on the basis of ECJ supremacy form binding precedents?

Remedies

All the UK statutory rights are defined as property rights (they are personal property) and remedies flow from that fact. Infringement of a property right is a tort and the general principles governing remedies in tort will apply, subject to any particular statutory provisions.

EU Directive 2004/48 on the enforcement of intellectual property rights harmonizes this area. Only a few statutory changes were necessary to arrange compliance with this—see the following section.

The remedies available for the non-statutory rights are governed by specific case-law and the general principles governing remedies in tort.

General principles are set out in the following sections, with specific applications dealt with in relation to individual rights.

Damages

The basic tortious principle (delictual principle in Scotland) of putting the claimant in the position they would have been in had the tort not been committed can be applied in two ways:

- assume the claimant exercised their monopoly and calculate losses to it, for example lost sales;
- assume the claimant was willing to license their right and calculate losses on the basis of what a reasonable royalty for the defendant's activities would have been.

Claimants can choose which basis to use. When calculating actual losses, the doctrines of remoteness and foreseeability apply, and can limit the types of loss that can be claimed.

Some rights provide for additional damages in the case of flagrant breaches. In addition, there is an important general effect of the **Enforcement Directive (2004/48/EC)**:

Intellectual Property (Enforcement, etc) Regulations 2006 (SI 2006/1028), reg 3

3.—Assessment of damages

(1) Where in an action for infringement of an intellectual property right the defendant knew, or had reasonable grounds to know, that he engaged in infringing activity, the damages awarded to the claimant shall be appropriate to the actual prejudice he suffered as a result of the infringement.

(2) When awarding such damages—

(a) all appropriate aspects shall be taken into account, including in particular—

(i) the negative economic consequences, including any lost profits, which the claimant has suffered, and any unfair profits made by the defendant; and

(ii) elements other than economic factors, including the moral prejudice caused to the claimant by the infringement; or

(b) where appropriate, they may be awarded on the basis of the royalties or fees which would have been due had the defendant obtained a licence.

The aspects of this that extend the law on damages are the possibilities of including 'unfair profits' and compensation for 'moral prejudice'.

An account of profits

This remedy is available for all the rights. Claimants can choose this as an alternative to damages and can obtain disclosure from the defendant to help them to make that choice. The problem with claiming an account is that the defendant may be able to prove substantial expense items on the profit and loss calculation, reducing the amount recovered, so this is only appropriate where the claimant can confidently estimate both income and expenses in the defendant's operation.

Final and interim injunctions (final and interim interdicts in Scotland)

Where a defendant has carried on infringing activity, an injunction will normally be awarded at the trial of the action (a final injunction) restraining infringement. Individuals, companies, and company officers can be punished by contempt of court proceedings (possibly leading to a fine or imprisonment) where they or the company are in breach of an injunction.

The court has a discretion to restrain infringing activity before the trial by granting interim injunctions (formerly 'interlocutory' injunctions). 'Quia timet' injunctions can be obtained to restrain activity that has not yet happened, as long as it is threatened or intended.

The leading case is *American Cyanamid*:

> **American Cyanamid v Ethicon [1975] AC 396 (HL)**
>
> An interim injunction should be granted where:
>
> - there is a serious issue to be tried (a test concerning the strength of the claimant's case);
> - damages to the claimant awarded at trial would not be an adequate remedy;
> - the 'balance of convenience' lies in favour of granting an injunction.
>
> To obtain an injunction, claimants must give a 'cross-undertaking' to the court to compensate the defendant for any loss suffered as a result of the injunction, should the trial court not grant a permanent injunction.

Judges normally combine the requirement that damages are not an adequate remedy and the balance of convenience into a global balancing test that considers also the adequacy of a payment under the cross-undertaking in compensating the defendant if wrongly injuncted, and both sides' abilities to pay damages/compensation.

Damages will generally be regarded as an inadequate remedy where damage to **goodwill** or reputation is involved, or damage may include items not recoverable by reason of remoteness (eg lost business development opportunities). Interim injunctions will often be appropriate in trade mark, passing-off, and trade secrets cases.

The 'serious issue' test has been criticized by academics and judges as being too easy to meet, resulting in injustice to defendants.

> **Series 5 Software v Clarke [1996] 1 All ER 853 (HC)**
>
> Where it is possible to come to a view on the merits of the case at an early stage (without conducting a 'mini trial'), the court should do so and include the relative strengths of the parties' cases in the overall balancing act. This is not inconsistent with **American Cyanamid**.

The *Series 5* interpretation of the law has not been overruled by subsequent cases, but has not been expressly applied either.

> **Guardian Media Groups v Associated Newspapers 2000 WL 331035**
>
> The **Series 5** approach was not suitable where it was not possible to come to a clear view of the merits of the parties' cases at an early stage.

✅ *Looking for extra marks?*

When considering if an interim injunction is appropriate, always also consider if the *Series 5* approach would be applicable.

In specific cases, the strength of the claimant's case on the balance of probabilities is definitely recognized as a relevant factor.

Human Rights Act 1998, s 12

12.—Freedom of expression

(1) This section applies if a court is considering whether to grant any relief which, if granted, might affect the exercise of the Convention right to freedom of expression.

...

(3) No such relief is to be granted so as to restrain publication before trial unless the court is satisfied that the applicant is likely to establish that publication should not be allowed.

Where the interim injunction will effectively provide a final remedy, as where a limited duration restricted covenant is being enforced, a similar approach is taken—see Chapter 6 on trade secrets. In these cases, the court must do the best job it can of assessing the likelihood of success for the claimant's case at trial.

Delivery-up of materials, etc

The statutory rights all have a remedy, at the discretion of the court, that items the sale or use of which would infringe the rights, and related items such as the tooling or software necessary to make them, can be delivered up to the claimant. Alternatively, the defendant can be ordered to destroy them and confirm this on oath. The court has a discretion what to do with items delivered up in this way—destruction will not necessarily be ordered.

This type of remedy has also been ordered in trade secrets and passing-off cases as part of the court's inherent powers to give remedies.

Procedural remedies

The use of the court's procedural powers to order the disclosure of evidence, to allow the search of premises, and to freeze a defendant's assets, sometimes even before proceedings have started, is common in some types of IP action, for example against software pirates.

The free movement of goods under EU law

The EU Treaty provisions for the **free movement of goods** contained in **Arts 26–29 of the Treaty on the Functioning of the Internal Market (TFEU)** can impact on the enforceability of IP rights. The ECJ has ruled that IP rights are not contrary to the EU Treaties, but that the enforcement of IP rights may be inconsistent with the free movement of goods provisions.

SA Cnl-Sucal NV v Hag GF AG ('HAG II') (C-10/89) [1990] 3 CMLR 571

The **owner** of an intellectual property right cannot enforce that right to prevent goods from being imported into or sold in a Member State where those particular goods have been placed on the market within the European Economic Area (EEA) by or with the consent of the rights owner.
  But where there is no such consent, rights can be enforced.

This is the doctrine of 'exhaustion of rights'—once there has been consent to marketing in the EEA (and the owner had a chance to extract a fee or deny entry at that point), rights can no longer be enforced in relation to those particular goods.

In more recent statutes this rule is reflected in statutory wording, but this is not the case with the **Patents Act 1977**. The detailed application of this rule is discussed in relation to each right.

The mere fact that the copies were marketed with the consent of the copyright owner outside the EEA does not imply consent to marketing them within the EEA, so rights owners can prevent 'official' goods being sold between economic blocs by what is known as 'parallel importing'—buying legal goods intended for one market and selling them in another market to take advantage of regional price differences.

Revision tip

The free movement of goods provides a defence to an action for infringement; the absence of the defence does not mean there is infringement. For each right, decide first whether, and if so how, it can be infringed by dealing in 'genuine' goods—which is where the defence is likely to apply. The defence can only apply to fake or pirate goods if there has been consent to their marketing (perhaps as part of a settlement with an infringer).

#2
Copyright

Key facts

Copyright arises whenever a *work* is created under *qualifying conditions*. The **Copyright, Designs and Patents Act 1988 (CDPA)** defines eight types of work (see Figure 2.1).

Works qualify for protection with reference to the nationality of the author or the place of publication—most countries of the world are qualifying countries.

Copyright is infringed by copying, broadcasting, etc the whole or a substantial part of a work (**primary infringement**) or dealing in infringing copies of a work (**secondary infringement**).

Figure 2.1 The eight types of work

Authorial works—must be **original**

> *literary, dramatic,* and *musical* works must be recorded in material form

> there is no need for *artistic* works to be recorded

Can be infringed by re-creating their content in a different work

Entrepreneurial works or **neighbouring rights**—need not be original, but must not be copies of other such works

> *sound recordings, films, broadcasts,* and the typographical arrangement of *published editions*

Can only be infringed by reprographic copying

Overview, history, and theory

Copyright can be justified from a number of different theoretical perspectives:

- The **authors' rights** approach favoured in civil law jurisdictions holds that the right of authors to exploit their work economically is a fundamental right.

- The approach in common law jurisdictions has been to regard authors as 'workers of the mind' who are entitled to be paid for their labour like any other worker.

- Common law jurisdictions have also developed theories that we should reward authors if we enjoy using their work—based on ideas of fairness and also on the idea that this will provide an incentive for them to produce more works.

- According to economic theory (see Chapter 1) creative works are 'common goods' and thus the creation of a legal right is required in order to ensure a market in creative goods develops.

The scope and reach of copyright has increased over the past century, as has a process of harmonization via international treaties. The most important treaties are the **Berne Convention** (which deals with **authorial works**) and the **Rome Convention** (which deals with sound recordings and performers' rights). These seek to harmonize protection at a basic level. In addition, the **Agreement on Trade-Related Aspects of Intellectual Property (TRIPs)** requires signatory states to observe the provisions of the **Berne Convention** and to provide protection in relation to performers, producers of phonograms, and broadcasters.

UK copyright law is influenced by EU Directives in a piecemeal fashion, with separate Directives addressing different areas of activity. The following Directives have been implemented mainly by amendment to the **CDPA**:

- satellite broadcasting—**Directive 93/83/EC**;

- **databases**—**Directive 96/9/EC**;

- conditional access (deals with protection of encrypted signals, eg satellite TV)—**Directive 98/84/EC**;

- the **Information Society Directive** (deals with infringing acts and defences, but has more far-reaching implications)—**Directive 2001/29/EC**;

- rental and lending—**Directive 2006/115/EC** (makes renting out copies of works an infringing act, which it previously was not);

- duration of copyright—**Directive 2006/116/EC**;

- protection of **computer programs**—**Directive 2009/24/EC**.

See Chapter 1 for the legal implications of the implementation of EU Directives. In *Infopaq* (discussed below under 'Originality') and subsequent cases the ECJ has interpreted the body of EU law in this area as meaning that all aspects of authorial copyright are now subject to an autonomous EU law interpretation—including aspects not explicitly addressed by any

Directive, such as the nature of copyright works, the global test for originality, and the question of how much of a work must be taken (if the whole work is not copied) for there to be infringement.

How copyright arises

The authorial works

It has been argued that the effect of ECJ decisions following *Infopaq* is that anything, regardless of whether it fits into a particular category of work, must be protected if it amounts to the author's 'own intellectual creation'.

> **Bezpečnostní softwarová asociace—Svaz softwarove ochrany v Ministerstvo kultury [2011] ECDR 3 (ECJ)**
>
> **HELD:** Following *Infopaq*, if the graphical user interface of a program constituted the author's intellectual creation then it can be protected by copyright.

Bezpečnostní is also discussed in Chapter 3.

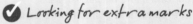 *Looking for extra marks*

The question of which created things amount to protectable works is now a matter of EU law, but it is unclear how the ECJ will approach this issue when difficult subject matter comes before it: some EU states protect fragrances by copyright, for example. See Key Debate 'The things that amount to work and the test for originality'.

This must be borne in mind when considering the categorization of works. The existing UK law on protectable works is discussed later, but it can no longer be said that a created thing that does not fall within any of the eight categories of the Act is not protected. In such a case, EU law will also have to be considered.

According to the Act, copyright only exists in literary, dramatic, and musical works if they are 'recorded in a material form' (s 3(2)). There is no such requirement for artistic works, as these are defined in terms of the physical product of the creative process, whereas the other works can exist in the mind without being recorded. Note that the recording does not have to be by the author or at the time of creation of the work: a piece of music developed solely through performance will be recorded (and copyright will arise) when a sound recording is made of its performance.

Originality is often, but not always, the issue that determines whether copyright exists in a creation, so many of the cases mentioned are summarized in the section 'Originality'.

The statutory definitions

Notwithstanding the impact of EU law noted above, the case-law interpreting these is discussed below to illustrate the range of protectable works.

Literary works (s 3(1))

Literary works are defined as *including* tables and compilations and 'words intended to be spoken or sung to music' (lyrics). Case-law has held that anything recording information is included, thus the following have been held to be literary works:

- telegraphic codes;

D P Anderson v Lieber Code Co [1917] 2 KB 469

A telegraphic code, consisting of a table matching sequences of electrical pulses to the letters of the alphabet, was a literary work.

- electrical circuit diagrams;

Anacon v Environmental Research [1994] FSR 659

Both the 'schematic' and the 'net list', created when an electrical circuit is designed, are literary works. Both works record which contact of which component connects to which contact of other components, rather than any particular layout of the circuit on a circuit board.

- examination papers consisting of a selection of pre-existing questions (*London University v Tutorial Press* [1916]);
- compilations of data (if these do not amount to databases as defined)—*Football League v Littlewoods* [1959] (see 'Originality' and Chapter 3).

Literary works are defined to include databases, computer programs, and preparatory material for computer programs—dealt with in Chapter 3.

Dramatic works (s 3(1))

The definition of dramatic works 'includes a work of dance or mime' but does not define drama. A script for a stage play or a film (known as a 'screenplay') will be a dramatic work, not a literary work.

In *Norowzian v Arks (No 2)* [2000] the Court of Appeal held that a film of a dance created using the editing technique of 'jump-cutting' (so that the dance seen on the screen could not be physically performed by a dancer) was a dramatic work, as it involved movement and could be displayed to an audience. An interesting aspect of the judgments is that one reason for this

How copyright arises

finding was the need to comply with the requirements of the Berne Convention to protect 'works of cinematography' as authorial works. To achieve this, films (at least where they involved original cinematography) would have to be treated as a type of dramatic work. See 'Films and their uneasy position in UK copyright law'.

Norowzian raises the possibility that film directors who invest creative skill in aspects of their work such as photography, soundtrack synchronization, and editing may acquire dramatic copyright in the result. Only creative films will stand a chance of acquiring dramatic status in this way—a security video will not be a dramatic work.

Musical works (s 3(1))

There is no definition of music, although s 3(1) states that it does not include lyrics. There are no cases in which the concept of 'music' has been seriously considered as no problem cases have yet arisen. In *Sawkins v Hyperion Records* [2004] it was held that a musical work had been created by transcribing an old work into modern musical notation while leaving the music unchanged—this decision was controversial, but the controversy centres on the notion of originality.

Artistic works

Artistic works are defined in s 4 and involve a number of sub-definitions. The sub-definitions are exhaustive—if something is not one of the following, it is not an artistic work:

Graphic works, photographs, sculptures, and collages 'irrespective of artistic quality'

Graphic works are further defined to include drawings, paintings, diagrams, maps, charts, plans and engravings, etchings, lithographs, woodcuts, and similar works. Photographs are defined to require the recording of light or other radiation, and do not include a still image from a film.

The words 'irrespective of artistic quality' mean that technical and engineering drawings are protectable by copyright provided they are original (see 'Originality'—it does not require any artistic intent or skill).

The difficult areas in relation to artistic works are works that are created in three dimensions—sculptures, collages, works of artistic craftsmanship, and (at the borderline between two- and three-dimensional objects) engravings.

Metix v Maughan [1997] FSR 718

The High Court moved away from the previous approach of defining sculpture with reference to how something was made, and suggested a definition: 'a three dimensional work by an artist's hand'.

Lucasfilm v Ainsworth [2011], which was a Supreme Court case, cemented this change of approach and developed it. The court proposed a 'multifactorial approach' that placed great weight on the need for the creator to have intended their work to be art—to be appreciated for its appearance.

Cases on engravings have held that the word 'engraving' includes anything made by forming a surface and the objects made by taking impressions from it. This clearly includes things made for artistic purposes, but also includes industrial objects.

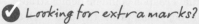

✅ Looking for extra marks?

The requirement for artistic intent in sculptures has been criticized as being contrary to the 'irrespective of artistic quality' requirement—but can be justified by interpreting 'quality' as meaning 'merit', so the question 'Is it art?' may be asked, but not the question 'Is it good art?'. Even this is a departure from the courts' earlier approach, which was to avoid all forms of artistic judgement. It is possible that when cases on engravings and collage come before it, the Supreme Court may clarify the role of artistic intention in those areas.

Works of architecture

Works of architecture are defined to include architectural models.

Works of artistic craftsmanship

The original policy basis for the 'works of artistic craftsmanship' category was to protect work of the type produced by the arts and crafts movement. A precise definition of this category has proved elusive.

George Hensher Ltd v Restawhile Upholstery (Lancs) Ltd [1976] AC 64

FACTS: A hand-made mock-up for an item of furniture intended to be mass-produced was asserted to be a work of artistic craftsmanship. The parties had conceded that it involved craftsmanship (although the court doubted this).

HELD: To be protected an item must have artistic character. There was no consensus on what this meant, although there was on the conclusion that the mock-up lacked it.

The Supreme Court in *Lucasfilm* noted that this category was intended to encompass creations that would not qualify as sculptures, so the definition of art from that case cannot be used to assist with the composite phrase 'artistic craftsmanship'.

Originality

The question of what originality means was, until EU law intervened, a matter of case-law. The EU definition of originality is that something must be the author's 'own intellectual creation'—this appears in the **Software Directive (2009/24/EC)** and the **Database Directive (96/9/EC)**.

The EU 'intellectual creation' test

Infopaq International A/S v DanskeDagbladesForening [2009] was a case about infringement of copyright by taking (inter alia) headlines from literary works. The ECJ interpreted

How copyright arises

✱✱✱✱✱✱✱✱✱✱✱✱

the **Information Society Directive** (which states that copyright is infringed by taking 'part' of a work) by equating the question 'How much is part?' to the presence of originality in that part. It held that something amounted to 'part' of a work if it represented the author's own intellectual creation. The court referred to the selection and organization of the words in a newspaper headline as being aspects where intellectual creation could be demonstrated, so a newspaper headline *might* be original and entitled to copyright protection as a work on its own. Subsequent ECJ cases have confirmed that the test for originality is a matter of EU law and the same test applies to all types of authorial work.

The Court of Appeal followed this in *NLA v Meltwater (see 'Infringing acts')*, although it held that the 'intellectual creation' test is not inconsistent with traditional UK doctrine.

In *SAS Institute v World Programming* [2012], a case mainly about computer programs, the ECJ applied the concept of 'expression' from the Software Directive (see Chapter 3) to ordinary literary copyright. It held that copyright protects only 'the expression of the intellectual creation of the author'. The Court of Appeal subsequently followed and sought to explain this approach, proposing that the same underlying principles apply to all works, whether or not programs. The other side of the concept that copyright protects only expression is that it does not protect underlying ideas—the so-called 'idea–expression dichotomy'. The non-protection of underlying ideas is in the Software Directive but not other Directives.

SAS calls into question the finding in *NLA* that the EU approach to originality is the same as the previous UK one. But the ECJ cases are consistent with the previous UK approach in that only a small amount of input is required to get over the threshold of originality, and that the questions of originality and infringement by taking part are linked (see 'Infringing acts'). We await a clear indication of the type of mental activity that 'intellectual creation' involves and how it might differ from the traditional UK 'skill and labour' approach, and of how the ECJ will develop doctrine in relation to ideas and their expression.

✅ *Looking for extra marks?*

Make sure you always consider and apply the 'intellectual creation' test for originality, even though it is a good idea to refer to earlier UK cases based on the 'skill and labour' test as examples in specific situations not addressed in EU case-law.

The traditional UK 'skill and labour' test

While the EU case-law develops, previous UK cases are useful as a starting point for considering originality, but whether the intellectual creation test might give a different outcome should always be considered.

The traditional UK test is that a work must involve some **skill and labour** on the part of the author in order to be original.

Literary works

Walter v Lane [1900] AC 539

FACTS: A journalist recorded a political speech in shorthand notation, which was eventually published in a newspaper.

HELD: The journalist owned copyright in the report of the speech because he expended skill and labour in recording it (it would have been different if portable sound recorders had been available).

Very short texts have failed the originality test:

Francis Day and Hunter v Twentieth Century Fox [1940] AC 112

FACTS: The claimants owned copyright in a song, the title and a recurrent line of which was 'The man who broke the bank at Monte Carlo'.

HELD: They could not prevent use of that phrase in the title of a film as no skill and labour went into creating that phrase, which was hackneyed and unoriginal.

Musical works

Sawkins v Hyperion Records [2005] EWCA Civ 565, [2005] 1 WLR 3281

FACTS: Dr Sawkins claimed copyright in his transcriptions into current musical notation of the works of the seventeenth-century composer Lalande—although in some cases the underlying music was not altered in any way.

HELD: He owned copyright in his transcriptions, the court referring approvingly to *Walter v Lane* and distinguishing *Interlego*. Dr Sawkins had expended musical skill and labour in writing the scores.

Artistic works

Interlego v Tyco [1989] AC 217

FACTS: Slavish copies of earlier drawings of Lego bricks were hand-drawn.

HELD: They were not original, despite the draughtsmanship that went into their creation.

Antiquesportfolio.com v Rodney Fitch [2001] ECDR 5

HELD: Photographs of furniture were original because skill and labour went into arranging the furniture and lighting the scene.

How copyright arises

✳✳✳✳✳✳✳✳✳✳✳✳

Antiquesportfolio leaves open the status of snapshots where no thought or arrangement goes into the photograph, although some commentators have asserted that being in the right place at the right time is sufficient. There are no UK cases where copyright was denied for a photograph on the basis of lack of originality.

The nature of originality is discussed further in relation to infringement.

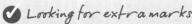

✅ *Looking for extra marks*

Some UK cases might not pass the EU originality test because intellectual work, but no creativity, went into them. Examples are *Walter v Lane*, the notion of being in the right place at the right time (photographs), and a line of cases involving compilations of data—see Chapter 3 for more detail.

Ownership and duration of authorial copyrights

The first **owner** is (ss 9–11)

- the author, who is the 'person who creates' the work; or
- (where the work was created in the course of employment) the author's employer.

The creator of a work is the person who provides the originality. Where more than one person is involved in a work's creation, they are joint authors (and so joint owners) if their contributions cannot be separated. If they can be separated, each owns the copyright in their part. Where a work is created by one contributor handing over to another, their contributions are likely to be treated as separate.

Ray v Classic FM Plc [1998] ECC 488

FACTS: Programme outlines and some playlists for a proposed classical music station were developed by R, then passed on to Classic, which did further work on R's output and used the result.

HELD: The contributions of R and the station were separate; therefore separate copyrights arose (so R's copyright was infringed).

In joint authorship cases there may well be a contract between the contributors which deals expressly with ownership.

Authorial copyright lasts for 70 years following the end of the calendar year of the author's death, or the last to die of joint authors. Where music and lyrics are written together, both copyrights expire on the day the one of longer duration would expire under the ordinary rules (ss 10A and 12(8)).

Computer-generated authorial works

The **CDPA** defines 'computer generated works' as being works where there is no human author (s 178), and in s 9(3) states that the owner of computer-generated authorial works is the person who makes the arrangements for them to be made. Note that most works created *using* computers will have a human author, so this provision is unlikely to apply.

Entrepreneurial works

As entrepreneurial works require no originality, in each case the **CDPA** specifies that no copyright exists in a film, sound recording, etc that is a copy of another film, etc. Such a provision is not necessary in the case of authorial works, as slavish copies will lack originality (*Interlego* discussed earlier).

Films and their uneasy position in UK copyright law

Films are defined as: 'a recording on any medium from which a moving image may by any means be reproduced' (s 5B). This will include film shot with a movie camera, but also films made entirely within a computer (as in the case of CGI-enhanced films). Film copyright includes the soundtrack (thus, if only the soundtrack of a film is copied, the film copyright will be infringed). This does not affect the copyright in any separate sound recording that may have been made and subsequently synchronized with the film.

Film copyright resembles copyright in authorial works in some respects: the duration is for the life of the director plus 70 years, the first owner is (or includes) the director (creative person not entrepreneur), and moral rights attach to the director. Yet films are not authorial works—originality is not required and film copyright can only be infringed by reprographic copying. In *Norowzian v Arks (No 1)* [1988], Mr Norowzian asserted his copyright as a film, but because the defendants had created their own film using Mr Norowzian's creative ideas and techniques, there was no infringement. Mr Norowzian therefore went on to claim that his film was a dramatic work in *Norowzian (No 2)*.

The reason that film copyright has this hybrid position is that the UK chose to protect films as entrepreneurial works, but has had to treat them like authorial works in order to comply with the **Berne Convention** on moral rights and with the EU **Duration Directive (2006/116/EC)** (ownership and duration). Since then, *Norowzian (No 2)* has introduced the argument that compliance with the Berne requirement that works of cinematography must be protected as authorial works could be achieved by extending the scope of dramatic copyright to include the artistic input of a cinematographer in a film.

The rights involved in film production

It is important to remember that dramatic copyright may protect the content of a film (script, dialogue, dance, stunts/fights). The rights of any performers involved will need to be taken into consideration. In addition, artistic works may have been created for the film in the form of sets, costume designs, etc. Often music is specially performed and recorded (sound recording copyright) or specially composed or arranged (musical copyright). All these copyrights and related rights will be infringed when the film is shown in a cinema, so the producer must obtain all the necessary rights. See Figure 2.2.

How copyright arises

✱✱✱✱✱✱✱✱✱✱

Figure 2.2 The combination of rights

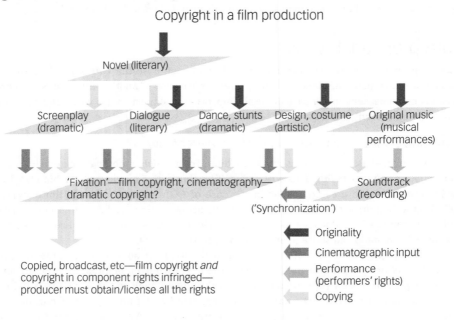

Copyright in a film production

Novel (literary)

Screenplay (dramatic) — Dialogue (literary) — Dance, stunts (dramatic) — Design, costume (artistic) — Original music (musical performances)

'Fixation'—film copyright, cinematography—dramatic copyright? — Soundtrack (recording)

('Synchronization')

Copied, broadcast, etc—film copyright *and* copyright in component rights infringed—producer must obtain/license all the rights

← Originality
← Cinematographic input
← Performance (performers' rights)
← Copying

✓ Looking for extra marks?

Remember that the directorial input (framing scenes, editing, etc) may be protected as dramatic content following *Norowzian (No 2)*, in addition to any dramatic content in the screenplay, dance routines, fights, etc.

Sound recordings

Sound recordings are defined in s 5A as 'a recording of sounds, from which the sounds may be reproduced' and also 'a recording of the whole or any part of an [authorial work] from which sounds reproducing the work or part may be produced'.

Always bear in mind that musical copyright may protect the content of the recording (though not in the case of, for example, a simple recording of birdsong) and that performers' rights may need to be dealt with.

Broadcasts

The definition of a broadcast in **CDPA, s 6** was amended to be consistent with the **Information Society Directive**. The definition embraces all forms of electronic transmission (conventional radio, cable and satellite broadcast, as well as 'webcasts') made to the public, including encrypted transmissions where decryption devices are available to the public. Only real-time transmissions and transmissions made at a time of the broadcaster's choosing are broadcasts as defined. Transmissions at a time chosen by the receiver are not broadcasts, so no broadcast is made when material is uploaded to a website from which it can be streamed or downloaded on demand by the user.

Broadcasts will often involve underlying copyright in the content, for which permission will need to be obtained (broadcasting is an infringing act). But a live broadcast of ordinary life (no music or dance, etc) will involve no underlying copyright. If it is also recorded at the time of filming, film copyright will arise.

Published editions

Section 8 defines published editions as the typographical arrangement of a published edition of the whole or any part of one or more literary, dramatic, or musical works. Typography is the arrangement of text on a page, choice of typeface and size, and so on. It will thus protect publishers from reprographic copying of their products even when there is no copyright in the underlying content (note that 'work' as defined in the Act is not the same thing as 'copyright work', so published edition copyright will arise in a new print of out-of-copyright material).

Duration and ownership of copyright in entrepreneurial works

These are set out in Table 2.1.

In all cases, time periods are calculated from the end of the calendar year in which the event happens—so copyrights always end on 31 December.

'Producer' is defined in s 178 as the person who undertakes the arrangement for the film or sound recording—that is, the entrepreneur, rather than any creative person involved.

Table 2.1 Duration and ownership of entrepreneurial works (ss 12–15A)

Right	Duration	Owner
Film	70 years from when the last of the principal director, author of screenplay or dialogue, or composer of specially created music dies	Producer *and* principal director
Sound recording	50 years from making or, if the recording is published or communicated to the public, 70 years from first publication or communication (50 years in the case of non-EEA authors)	Producer
Broadcast	50 years from broadcast	Broadcaster
Published edition	25 years from date of first publication	Publisher

Qualification for copyright protection

A work will only be protected by copyright if it qualifies for protection as set out in ss 153–156: if the author of the work is a citizen of a qualifying country, or the work was first published in or broadcast from a qualifying country, then it will be protected. 'Qualifying country' is defined as a country to which the CDPA *extends* or to which it has been *applied*.

The CDPA *extends* throughout the UK. Section 159 gives ministers the power to *apply* provisions of the Act to other countries. They have used this to apply the provisions as to qualification for copyright protection to all other countries that have signed up to the relevant convention (the Berne Convention for LDMA works and the Rome Convention for sound recordings) or offer reciprocal protection. In practice, this includes most countries for LDMA works and many in the case of sound recordings. Of course, these countries, following their treaty obligations, give copyright protection to the works of UK authors and to works first published in the UK. This reciprocal protection is crucial in making copyright effective internationally.

Rights of the copyright owner and infringement

Rights

The rights given by the CDPA have been amended to comply with the Information Society Directive, which requires EU states to give authors of original works and owners of neighbouring rights the 'reproduction right' (copying), the 'communication right' (broadcasting and making available on the internet), and the 'distribution right' (authorial works only covering first and subsequent sales of copies). The Act provides the distribution right for all types of work.

The CDPA creates two types of infringing act: primary and secondary. Primary infringing acts involve the initiation of infringing activity, whereas secondary infringing acts typically involve activity in relation to infringing copies of works or which assists infringement.

The Directive requires that these rights apply to works or parts of works; the Act says that the rights are infringed by doing an infringing act in relation to the work or a substantial part of it. Following *Infopaq* and subsequent ECJ cases, discussed earlier in relation to originality, the provisions in the CDPA on infringement must be interpreted so as to comply with EU law; thus the 'substantial part' must now be interpreted to mean the same thing as 'part' in the Information Society Directive, as that has been interpreted by the ECJ. The Court of Appeal acknowledged this in *SAS* (discussed under 'The EU "intellectual creation" test').

Infringing acts

The Act defines the detail of the rights in terms of the acts which, if carried out without the permission of the owner, amount to infringement of copyright.

Primary infringing acts

The primary infringing acts are as follows.

Copying (s 17)

The copy can be in any material form (which includes digital form). This includes transient copies. Thus, whenever you browse to a web page, you make copies of the text and images. (In *NLA v Meltwater* the ECJ confirmed that the 'transient copies' defence applied to ordinary acts of browsing to lawful material—dealt with under 'Defences to copyright infringement'.)

For entrepreneurial works, only reprographic copying infringes copyright. In *Norowzian v Arks (No 1)*, it was held that a film that had been made so as to reproduce aspects of the shooting and editing of the claimant's film was not copied.

In the case of authorial works, copying requires a *causal link* between the content of the claimant's work and the content of the defendant's work. Independent creation that results in the same features being present is not copying—a common situation where this arises is when both the original creator and alleged copyist draw on the same starting materials or operate within the same constraints. The chain of causation can be indirect—see Chapter 8 ('Designs') for an example of this. In the case of literary works, a computer program may be copied by writing a program that reproduces the functionality of the original, even though the copyist had no access to the original source code—see Chapter 3.

Issuing to the public (s 18)

This covers the first sale to the public in the European Economic Area (EEA) of a particular copy of a work—whether or not that copy was made with the consent of the copyright owner. The wording of s 18 reflects EU policy on the **free movement of goods** and the exhaustion of rights—see 'The free movement of goods under EU law' in Chapter 1. As issuing is a primary infringing act, there is no requirement for knowledge, unlike with the secondary infringing act of importing.

Performing or showing the work in public (s 19)

This covers both live performance and playing a recording or broadcast of a work to a public audience—but not doing so in private. The Information Society Directive is not concerned with live performances, but ECJ case-law has held that playing a recording to an audience is within the scope of the communication right and so the concept of the public from that right applies.

Communicating the work to the public (s 20)

If material is placed on the internet so that it is publicly accessible by downloading or streaming at a time chosen by the recipient, there is infringement by 'making available'

Rights of the copyright owner and infringement

✳✳✳✳✳✳✳✳✳✳✳✳

under s 20(2)(b). If the time is fixed by the person making it available, there is infringement by 'broadcasting' under s 20(2)(a).

A series of ECJ cases have established that communicating means transmission to an audience 'who are not present at the place where the transmission originates', so includes:

* making material available for download or streaming on the internet (file-sharers will often infringe in this way, and websites that provide assistance to them by hosting or linking to torrent files may also infringe as joint tortfeasors);
* showing live television broadcasts or playing recordings to a public audience (though UK law deals with this under s 19)—that is in these situations the communication originates where the original broadcast or recording was made, not where the playing equipment is;
* real-time broadcasting or webcasting;
* (controversially) hyperlinking (see the *GS Media* case below).

The public means 'a new public', that is a public not originally envisaged by the rights owner in relation to the source material that is communicated (*Rafael Hotels*). This has been held to include customers in a pub to whom broadcasts were shown, but not patients in a dental practice listening to the radio, and to include any communication by a technologically different means than that originally envisaged, such as when free-to-air broadcasts are streamed in real time over the internet.

GS Media BV v Sanoma Media Netherlands BV (C-160/15) (ECJ)

HELD: Providing a hyperlink to material is only an infringement of copyright if: the material linked to is not *lawfully* available on the World Wide Web; and the person providing the link has knowledge that the material linked to is not lawfully there. The court confirmed that linking is a 'communication' (a controversial finding) and that in such a situation this was to a 'new public' (see below).

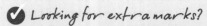 ✔ *Looking for extra marks?*

Communication is important and complex, and the ECJ approach has been criticized. It is worth reading more deeply, see Birgit Clark and Sabrina Tozzi, ' "Communication to the Public" under EU Copyright Law: An Increasingly Delphic Concept or Intentional Fragmentation?' (2016) 38(12) EIPR 715.

Making an adaptation of the work (s 21)

This is defined as changes between literary and dramatic forms, converting literary works to picture books, changes of musical key, and changing the language or format of programs and databases. Many ways of changing a work will not be adaptations as defined (eg an abridgment of a book for reading on radio) but will amount to copying in the ordinary sense.

Rental or lending of the work (s 18A)

Rental refers to hiring out copies; lending refers to the sort of thing public libraries do.

Secondary infringing acts

Secondary infringing acts require activity in relation to an *infringing copy* of a work. These are set out in **CDPA, ss 22–26**. They include dealing in copies of the work by selling, possessing in the course of trade, offering or exposing for sale, importing, and activities in relation to infringement, such as knowingly making premises or apparatus available. There are also infringing acts in **ss 296–299**, which deal with unlawful decryption of encrypted signals and subverting copy-protection measures.

An infringing copy is defined in **s 27** as a copy whose making, if it had been carried out in the UK, would have amounted to an infringing act. Thus UK law on copying and defences is applied to the making of the copy wherever it is made.

The key distinction between primary and secondary infringing acts is that there is a mental element to all the secondary infringing acts: the infringer must know or have reason to believe they were committing the act in relation to an infringing article or performance.

Pensher Security Doors v Sunderland City Council [2000] RPC 249

HELD: A mere suspicion is not a 'reason to believe'.

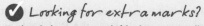 **Looking for extra marks?**

Each sale is a separate infringing act. A seller with a stock of infringing copies to get rid of can be given the requisite notice, whereupon they will satisfy the mental element; therefore any further sales will be infringing. This can put them out of pocket on their purchase of stock. They may have a remedy against the person who sold them the stock under contract law. Note that in relation to performers' rights and design right, there is a partial defence of 'innocent acquisition'—but not for copyright.

Infringing acts must take place within the jurisdiction

The **CDPA** *extends* to England, Wales, Scotland, and Northern Ireland (**s 157**), which means that infringement of the rights can only arise in relation to acts that occur there. It does not extend to foreign countries such as Portugal or Peru, so if objectionable activity occurs there, the local copyright law will apply. But what goes on overseas may be relevant to whether copyright exists (if works are created overseas) and to secondary infringement (if infringing articles are made overseas).

Infringement by taking part

The substantial part and entrepreneurial works

Here the issue will arise in relation to exact copying of a small part of a work. Section 17(4) states that copying a single frame of a film or broadcast is copying. In the matter of films, the England and Wales Cricket Board case now deals with this.

England and Wales Cricket Board Ltd v Tixdaq Ltd [2016] EWHC 575 (Ch)

FACTS: Extracts of sports broadcasts were communicated without permission, including key events such as wickets, where the section was only a few seconds long.

HELD: 'Substantial' in relation to a film referred to the investment that went into the film. As broadcasters who purchased rights to sports paid partly with a view to exploiting these key moments, they were a substantial part even though they lasted only a short time.

This principle can clearly be applied also to sound recordings. Watch out for appeals and ECJ referrals of this one!

Case-law has held that to infringe published edition copyright at least a whole page must be copied. There are no express rules about how much of a sound recording can be taken, but in the UK music industry, 'sampling fees' are paid where only a few seconds of a sound recording are used.

Infringement by taking part and authorial copyright

As copying can be indirect, infringement of an authorial work can arise from exact copying of a section of a work or from incorporation of features of one work into another.

The key ECJ cases have already been discussed in relation to originality. If the part taken is the author's intellectual creation, there will be infringement. In *SAS*, the ECJ held that copyright protects the expression of ideas, not the ideas themselves and that this concept applied to copyright generally, not just programs. The applicability of the 'idea–expression dichotomy' to UK law has long been a topic of debate. *SAS* has now clarified that. But while we wait for a non-software inexact copying case from the ECJ, the previous UK case-law is informative, though it no longer defines the law.

The leading UK case was *Designers Guild v Russell-Williams* [2000], a case concerning artistic copyright. The House of Lords confirmed that the doctrinal approach to the substantial part requirement was that the things taken from the original work must represent a substantial part of the original author's skill and labour. It also confirmed that, in assessing this, what is left behind and what is added to what is taken are ignored (in this respect the ECJ approach is similar). This is reflected in the saying that what matters is the quality of what has been taken, not the quantity.

Lord Hoffmann linked the substantial part requirement to the originality test and his judgment can be interpreted as requiring that 'the part taken should itself be a copyright work'.

Subsequent courts have found some difficulty with this aspect of Lord Hoffmann's reasoning:

Baigent & Leigh v Random House [2007] EWCA Civ 247, [2008] EMLR 7

FACTS: Dan Brown's novel *The Da Vinci Code* incorporated a view of history that had been put forward in an earlier non-fiction work.

HELD: The 'part taken should be a copyright work' test is not useful. While applying the 'substantial skill and labour' test, the court also expressed its finding in terms of the distinction between ideas and their expression: the historical theory (idea) may have been taken, but the way it had been expressed had not, so there was no infringement.

Many judges (like those in *Baigent*) have found idea/expression a useful distinction where only general aspects of a work are taken. It is known as the 'idea–expression dichotomy'. The US **Copyright Act of 1976** refers explicitly to ideas (not protected) and their expression (protected). These concepts are now part of EU law, though the detailed doctrine will not necessarily follow that of the US courts.

Defences to copyright infringement

The **CDPA** contains a large number of defences, many of which relate to very specific situations. The **Information Society Directive** deals with defences to all works apart from computer programs and databases (defences for these are dealt with in their Directives, discussed in Chapter 3). The EU states could not agree on defences, so, with the exception of one, all the defences listed in the Directive are optional—states may implement all, some, or no defences from the list, but no other defences.

Underlying the Directive and the Act is **Art 9 of the Berne Convention**, which permits defences only in certain special cases, provided the reproduction does not conflict with a normal exploitation of the work and does not unreasonably prejudice the legitimate interests of the author—the so-called 'Berne three-step test'.

✓ Looking for extra marks?

The difficulty in reaching agreement on this issue may reflect the cultural differences between states, which are reflected in the activities that are deemed so important as to warrant copyright defences. The list of allowed defences in the Directive illustrates the divergence of approaches taken by the EU states—each state lobbied for those defences that were important to it to be included.

The main generally applicable defences in the **CDPA** are:

- a defence covering temporary copies;
- the defences of 'fair dealing' for the purposes of:
    - private study or non-commercial research;
    - criticism, review, quotation, or reporting current events;

Defences to copyright infringement

- caricature, parody, or pastiche (the defences of quotation and of caricature, parody, or pastiche came into force on 1 October 2014 following lengthy consultation and deliberation).

- a non-statutory public interest defence that also follows 'fair dealing' principles;
- incidental inclusion.

There are also defences (some applying only to certain types of work) for copying by libraries and archives, in relation to public administration and education, and to enable reproduction to help visually impaired people. These defences are too extensive and detailed to describe here.

Defence for data carriers

The single defence required by the Directive is a defence covering temporary copies made in a communication network which are transient or incidental to a technical purpose (**CDPA**, s 28A). This covers copies made by 'buffering' (queuing) at network hubs (required to avoid data loss) but not cacheing by internet service providers (which is not technically necessary but improves the user experience). This defence was relevant to the *Meltwater* case.

> **Newspaper Licensing Agency Ltd and others v Meltwater Holding BV and others** [2011] EWCA Civ 890; *Public Relations Consultants Association Ltd v Newspaper Licensing Agency Ltd* [2014] EMLR 28 (ECJ)
>
> **FACTS:** The defendants crawled the web and scraped content from pages, re-presenting it to users in a searchable press 'cuttings' service.
>
> **HELD** by the Court of Appeal: The defence did not apply to the various acts of copying and making available involved in *creating the service*. The Supreme Court then referred the matter of infringement *by a user browsing the service* to the ECJ.
>
> **HELD** by the ECJ: The transient copies defence applies to copies made during browsing, both the onscreen copies and any *locally* cached copies generated by the web browser software.

This defence does not apply to computer programs or databases.

The private use defence, noted in the previous edition, has been repealed after the High Court held that it was arguably outside the scope of the allowable defence in the Information Society Directive.

The 'fair dealing' defences and the public interest defence

There are two stages to consider in relation to these defences: did the circumstances bring the activity within the scope of the defence, and was the use made of the work 'fair dealing'? The courts have been lenient in their interpretation of the purposes for which copying occurs, but have tended to be stricter when considering whether the dealing was fair.

Private study or non-commercial research (s 29)

Private study or non-commercial research does not include research undertaken for a commercial purpose such as technological research, or academic research as part of the activities of a university. It does include research by students for their own studies. Since 1 October 2014 this defence covers all works, not just authorial works—thus making life easier/legal for music, media, and film students (when combined with the introduction of a similar defence in relation to performers' rights—see Chapter 5).

Criticism or review (s 30(1))

The criticism or review must be of the copyright work or another work, and the defence only applies if there is a sufficient acknowledgement of the authorship of the work and where the work has been made available to the public.

The courts have adopted a wide interpretation of what 'another work' can include:

Pro Sieben Media AG v Carlton UK Television Ltd [1999] 1 WLR 605; Fraser-Woodward v BBC [2005] EWHC 472 (Ch), [2005] EMLR 22

HELD: Criticism of a genre of work ('chequebook journalism' and celebrity exploitation, respectively) is sufficient to ground the defence, subject to the dealing being fair.

Time Warner v Channel 4 [1994] EMLR 1

FACTS: A TV programme criticized director Stanley Kubrick's decision to withdraw his film *A Clockwork Orange* from UK distribution.

HELD: This was criticism of the film because the decision (and the criticism of it) was based on the artistic content of the film and the public reaction to that.

But in *Ashdown v Telegraph* [2001] publishing the manuscript of a politician's memoires was held not to be criticism of them *as a literary work*, although the political events concerned were critically reviewed.

Reporting current events (s 30(2))

In relation to reporting current events, as with criticism, there has to be a sufficient acknowledgement, but the work does not have to have been published. 'Current events' are not the same as news—anything that is a matter of current discussion in society is a current event.

Defences to copyright infringement

✳✳✳✳✳✳✳✳✳✳

> ### *Hyde Park v Yelland* [2001] Ch 143
>
> **FACTS:** The death of Diana, Princess of Wales, was still discussed in the press at the time of the alleged infringement.
>
> **HELD:** That element of public discussion made it a current event (despite having happened years previously).

Following this, issues that are discussed widely on the internet will also amount to current events (thus providing a defence for the mainstream media when they pick up the story). The printing of the memoires in *Ashdown* was held to be within the scope of current events as it concerned political negotiations that affected the current Parliament.

Most importantly, the defence does not apply to photographs—a specific exclusion intended to protect photojournalists (who would otherwise not have protection for their work).

Quotation (s 30(1ZA))

Copyright in a work is not infringed by the use of a quotation from the work (whether for criticism or review or otherwise) provided that—

(a) the work has been made available to the public;

(b) the use of the quotation is fair dealing with the work;

(c) the extent of the quotation is no more than is required by the specific purpose for which it is used; and

(d) the quotation is accompanied by a sufficient acknowledgement (unless this would be impossible for reasons of practicality or otherwise).

It is clear from this that there must be an underlying purpose for the quotation (presumably, other than quotation itself). What is not clear is what things will be considered suitable purposes for quotation—this will be a matter for judicial interpretation. Potentially, this defence will help bloggers and the like, who routinely quote material for the purposes of argument rather than criticism. The defence can apply to all forms of work, not just text, so artistic works and films may be 'quoted'.

Caricature, parody, or pastiche (s 30A)

The Act does not define the terms 'caricature', 'parody', or 'pastiche', so that will be a matter for the judges. It is possible for the courts to interpret the terms more narrowly than any EU law interpretation, but not more broadly. The ECJ has reviewed this area in *Deckmyn*.

> ### *Deckmyn v Vandersteen* (C-201/13)
>
> **HELD:** A parody must bring to mind the original work while being clearly different in some way, but whether intellectual creation has gone into the parody is irrelevant. A parody must have a humorous effect.

Note that there is no equivalent defence to an action for derogatory treatment—see Chapter 4.

The public interest defence

Before the CDPA was passed, a defence outside the statutory framework of the then Act was recognized:

Lion Laboratories v Evans [1985] QB 526

FACTS: A whistle-blower published internal documents from the manufacturer of breathalyzers, which showed that the results could be unreliable. He was sued for copyright infringement (and breach of confidence).

HELD: There was a defence as the reproduction of the material was in the public interest (specifically the public interest in a fair criminal justice system).

This defence is also used in relation to confidential information, and the public interest has been held to include the reporting of wrongdoing, public health and safety, and similar matters.

This defence was thought to be retained by CDPA, s 171(3); however, this was questioned in *Hyde Park*, although a form of public interest defence has been reinstated as a result of the decision in *Ashdown*. The Court of Appeal in *Ashdown* held that in 'rare cases' where the existing statutory defences did not adequately protect the right of freedom of expression (the Human Rights Act 1998 had recently been passed), the public interest defence would be available. It is not clear that *Ashdown* reinstated the defence in its former scope, but it did extend the notion of the public interest to include respect for human rights under the European Convention on Human Rights (ECHR).

'Fair dealing'

'Dealing' means anything done in relation to a work that would otherwise amount to infringement. 'Fairness' means that the amount used (how much is copied) and the way it is used (how widely it is published) must be no more than is fairly required in order to achieve the purpose of research, reporting, quotation, etc under which a defence is claimed. So, for example, a critical review needs to quote text; exact words are needed to report events. But the large sections of text that were reproduced in *Ashdown* went beyond what would have been needed for political comment, therefore the reporting defence failed. *Time Warner* is an example of the court being more lenient—over 20 minutes of a film were reproduced during a critical TV documentary, yet this was held to be fair.

Where the public interest defence is asserted, the courts have applied fair dealing principles in relation to achieving the public interest purpose (so a public interest defence failed in *Ashdown* also). They also refer to the ECHR and the human rights doctrine of proportionality.

In *Deckmyn*, the ECJ looked at the question of what parodies are permissible in terms of the fundamental right of freedom of expression and stated that this must be balanced against the property and moral rights of the owners/authors.

Incidental inclusion

This defence applies to all categories of work, but only where they are included incidentally in an artistic work, sound recording, film, or broadcast.

Football Association Premier League v Panini UK [2003] EWCA Civ 995, [2004] 1 WLR 1147

FACTS: The defendants published football cards displaying players and made sure that each player displayed their team logo on their shirt. Permission was obtained in relation to copyright in the photographs.

HELD: The fact that the depiction of the logo was an important part of the choice of photograph indicated that the inclusion was not incidental, so copyright _in the logos_ was infringed.

In the case of musical works or lyrics, the defence is not available if the material is included deliberately—_FAPL v Panini_ indicates that this principle is applied to other works as well.

The defence potentially covers photographs that include public sculptures or buildings (architectural works), sound recordings that happen to include background music, and so on.

'Innocent infringement' defence to damages only

If the infringer can show that they were unaware that copyright existed in the work, they can still be subject to an injunction, but not damages—s 97(1). Note that this applies even to primary infringers—secondary infringers will, in this situation, also no doubt lack the necessary mental element.

Defences—theoretical basis

The various theoretical bases for having copyright do not take into account the possibility that other individual rights, or the social benefit of other activities, may be of equal or greater importance. This matters if those rights and interests come into conflict with copyright. Thus, all the major and minor defences noted represent a competing right or public interest. The requirement for fairness in the fair dealing defences illustrates one way of attempting to strike a balance between the competing rights.

An economic analysis shows that defences can also be justified on the ground of 'market failure'—where it is not possible for potential copyright users to negotiate a licence because the transaction would be too small, for example.

Specific remedies for copyright infringement

In addition to the usual remedies available in IP actions (see Chapter 1) the following important remedies are provided by the **CDPA**:

- additional damages for flagrant infringement—s 97;
- delivery-up of infringing articles or things for making them, copy protection avoidance equipment, etc—s 99;
- a right for copyright owners to seize infringing articles from public display other than in shops or on vehicles—s 100.

Exploitation of copyright

Normally an author will not license or assign all the rights that copyright gives them; rather, they will carve up the rights so that they can be more effectively exploited. For example, the film rights to a novel are best exploited by a film producer, the book publishing rights by a book publisher, and so on.

Unlike the registered rights, which can only be assigned as a whole, it is possible to assign any defined part of the rights of a copyright owner. This is commonly done for the 'film rights' to a literary work, for example. It is also common for rights to be licensed, on terms that can vary from a short-term, non-exclusive licence to an exclusive licence for the full term of copyright.

Any assignment or exclusive licence of copyright must be in writing and signed by both parties. However, a contract (even an oral contract) may involve a term (express or implied) that copyright will be assigned—in which case the courts will grant a mandatory injunction requiring it to be assigned. These situations are known as 'equitable assignments' of copyright as the law regards the assignee as the owner in equity but not the legal owner.

In the case of the music industry and (to a lesser extent) other industries, sophisticated collective licensing schemes have grown up. Authors join societies that offer licences of the works to anyone who applies, while enforcing copyright against any infringer who has not purchased a licence. In the UK, the Performing Rights Society (which licenses the public broadcasting and performance of musical works) and the Mechanical-Copyright Protection Society (which licenses the making of sound recordings of musical works) operate under the brand 'PRS for Music' to offer a more comprehensive service to users. Phonographic Performance Ltd (PPL) licenses sound recording copyright for broadcast, etc on behalf of record companies.

Note that the 'performing right' is part of the copyright in a work and is different from 'performers' rights', which are addressed in Chapter 4. Musicians' performers' rights are licensed alongside the sound recording copyright by virtue of the contracts that performers sign with recording companies.

This system is used whenever music is played on the radio or in a public place such as a shop, or when a band plays covers in a pub. As a result of agreements between national collecting societies, a global repertoire is available.

Artist's re-sale right and publication right

As a result of EU Directive 2001/29/EC, implemented by the Artist's Resale Right Regulations 2006, authors of some artistic works ('works of graphic or plastic art') have a right to receive a royalty on subsequent sales of the work. The right also applies to copies of works that were produced in limited numbers, but not all copies.

Publication right applies where a work is published for the first time after copyright has expired and lasts 25 years. This was introduced by the **Term Directive (93/98/EEC)** and is implemented in the **Duration of Copyright and Rights in Performances Regulations 1995**.

(✱) Key cases

Case	Facts	Principle
Copyright in 'cinematography' and films, infringement		
Norowzian v Arks (Nos 1 and 2) [1999] EMLR 57, [2000] ECDR 205	N filmed a dancer performing a range of movements, then used a process of 'jump-cutting' to produce a finished film that did not record movement that could be physically performed. A made their own film for a TV advertisement that used a similar technique.	(No 1) Infringement of copyright in film and the other entrepreneurial works requires reprographic copying, so film copyright was not infringed. (No 2) Dramatic works must involve movement that can be performed. N's film did, as it could be displayed to an audience, so it was a dramatic work. This interpretation may satisfy the requirements of the **Berne Convention** that 'cinematographic works' be protected as authorial works. A had not infringed dramatic copyright as they had taken the jump-cutting idea, but not a substantial part of N's dramatic work.
Artistic works—sculptures		
Lucasfilm v Ainsworth [2011] UKSC 39, [2012] 1 AC 208	A had created three-dimensional models from which the storm trooper helmets used in the *Star Wars* films were made. He subsequently used these to make replica models for enthusiasts without permission of Lucasfilm. Lucasfilm asserted copyright in the models, so needed to show that they were sculptures (see Chapter 8 ('Designs') for why this was the relevant question).	The helmets used in the film were not sculptures. To be a sculpture a 'multi-factorial test' should be adopted as set out by Mann J at first instance: – regard should be had for what is ordinarily regarded as sculpture, while recognizing that some modern art may not be so recognized, yet be protected; – no judgement is to be made about artistic worth; – sculpture should have, as part of its purpose, a visual appeal in the sense that it might be enjoyed for that purpose alone (even if it has other purposes). Thus the artistic intention of the author is of paramount importance.

Case	Facts	Principle
Infringement of authorial copyright and originality of short literary works		
Infopaq International A/S v Danske Dagblades Forening (C-5/08) [2009] ECR I-6569)	D used scanners and software to collect headlines and extracts from hard-copy news and feature articles published by I and others. The full text was deleted once the headlines and extracts had been selected. Subscribers to D's service could search the extracts for keywords of interest to them. Some of the headlines were written separately from the articles by a sub-editor.	Some of the separately written headlines could amount to literary works in their own right as they involved intellectual creativity in capturing the essence of the article. Where headlines were not separately written, some of them would amount to a part of the whole work as required for infringement under the **Information Society Directive**. The test for this was whether they involved the author's intellectual creation, which also applied to the extracts. In both cases, extracts as short as 11 words *could* be protectable if the test was met. D infringed by copying and making available the headlines and extracts and the 'transient copies' defence did not apply to any stage of the process, including the temporary use of the full text scans.
General de Autores y Editores de España (SGAE) v Rafael Hoteles SL (C-306/05) [2006] ECR I-11519, [2007] ECDR 2	RH sent television broadcasts to guests by a network connecting the rooms, and were accused of infringement by 'communicating to the public'.	This amounted to communication as the recipients were not present at the place the transmission originated (which was the place of broadcast). It was 'to the public' as the hotel guests were not envisaged as recipients of the original broadcasts by the rights owners when they gave permission to the broadcaster.
Designers Guild v Russell-Williams [2000] 1 WLR 2416	DG had created a design called 'Ixia' for wallpaper, consisting of flowers on top of red-and-white stripes drawn as if by brushstrokes. R-W's design for fabric also contained these features, though the detailed implementation was different (different flowers, drawn to a different relative scale, and so on).	The Court of Appeal should not go behind the trial judge's finding of fact where these were the legally relevant facts. The 'substantial part' test requires an analysis of the amount of the original author's skill and labour that went into the creation of the aspects of D's work that are proved to be copied from C's work. This is the same test as for the originality of a work. The trial judge had not asked himself a significantly different question, so his finding of infringement should stand. Consideration of whether ideas or their expression had been taken were not inconsistent with this. High-level ideas are unlikely to involve literary or artistic skill and labour, nor are banal or commonplace ideas. But taking a sufficient quantity of the detailed ideas in a work can amount to infringement. The 'idea–expression dichotomy' is not part of the law and the courts should apply the substantial part test.

Key debates

✳✳✳✳✳✳✳✳✳

Case	Facts	Principle
SAS Institute Inc v World Programming Ltd [2013] EWCA Civ 1482, [2012] ECDR 22	W wrote software that was intended to be compatible with the SAS software, so reproduced the keywords and syntax of the commands from the SAS programming language in its software. W also wrote a user manual which described the commands of the language and their syntax. SAS asserted that copyright in their software and manual had been infringed by W's software and manual.	Reproducing the key words, syntax, and options of an individual command did not infringe any literary copyright in the SAS manual because the individual commands were not expressions of intellectual creation. It was possible that the combination and ordering of these elements when writing the manual might involve intellectual creation and so be protectable (that was for the referring court). The Court of Appeal subsequently endorsed and applied these principles.
Ashdown v Telegraph Group Ltd [2001] EWCA Civ 1142, [2002] Ch 149	The former leader of the Liberal Democratic Party had punted a draft of his memoires around publishers with a view to publication. A copy was leaked to the *Telegraph* newspaper, which published extended extracts without permission. The extracts dealt with the possible inclusion of A in the government under the Parliament that was still current at the time of publication.	As it involved the current Parliament, A's possible involvement in government was a matter of public interest and a current event. However, even if that were not the case, the public interest defence would apply in principle to protect the journalist's freedom of expression, as to which ECHR principles applied. The cases where this defence would 'trump' the statutory defences would be very rare. The amount of the memoires used was more than that needed to comment on events or exercise freedom of expression so was not fair dealing: the *Telegraph* could claim neither the statutory nor the extra-statutory defence.

⑨⑨ Key debates

Topic	The things that amount to 'work' and the test for originality
Author	Eleonora Rosati
Standpoint	Argues that *Infopaq* has dictated a harmonized test for originality and that the subsequent ***Bezpečnostní softwarová asociace*** case further dictates that all works involving intellectual creation (regardless of categorization issues) should be protected.

Source	'Originality in a Work, or a Work of Originality: The Effects of the Infopaq Decision' (2011) 33(12) EIPR 746–755
Author	Jonathan Griffiths
Standpoint	Argues that an EU approach will have to be developed and notes that artistic works will, like literary works, be judged by their content, not their manner of expression.
Source	'Dematerialisation, Pragmatism and the European Copyright Revolution' (2013) 33(4) *Oxford Journal of Legal Studies* 767–790

Topic	Does the CDPA deal with photographs and films rationally?
Author	Richard Arnold
Standpoint	Argues for photographs to be protected by both an authorial right (protecting original photographic art but not mere snaps) and a neighbouring right like films (protecting the fixation regardless of any originality, but only from reprographic copying). Also that the cinematographic content of films should be protected by an authorial copyright.
Source	'Copyright in Photographs: A Case for Reform' (2005) 27(9) EIPR 303–305

Topic	Are the defences to copyright infringement adequate to protect freedom of expression?
Author	Christina J Angelopoulos
Standpoint	*Ashdown* has not properly brought a defence of freedom of expression into UK copyright law.
Source	'Freedom of Expression and Copyright: The Double Balancing Act' [2008] 3 IPQ 328–353

(?) Exam questions

Problem question

Kevin is a renowned photographer from Sheffield whose work has been published in galleries around the world. One photograph from his most recent collection is of an artist working at an easel in the middle of a busy shopping centre. Kevin recently saw a TV advertisement for a chocolate bar that is based on an artist in the middle of a busy shopping centre eating a chocolate bar. He complained about this to the advertiser and on his blog, and included a still image of the advertisement, which he captured from the online version of the advertisement. Kevin's blog attracted attention from art critics, and the *Sunday Globe* magazine has just published a report on the dispute, including a copy of Kevin's photograph.

Exam questions

✳✳✳✳✳✳✳✳✳

Has Kevin's copyright been infringed by the advertiser, and has Kevin or the *Sunday Globe* infringed copyright in the blog and the report?

See the Outline Answers section in the end matter for help with this question.

Essay question

UK copyright law does not adequately protect modern forms of artistic expression. Discuss.

 Online Resource Centre

To see an outline answer to this question visit www.oup.com/lawrevision/

#3

Computer programs and databases

Key facts

Computer programs and **databases** are types of literary **work** for which EU Directives (the **Software Directive (91/250/EEC)** and the **Database Directive (96/9/EC)**) set special rules, which are implemented in the **CDPA**. In addition, the **Database Directive** provides for a separate right in databases: database right (known as the *sui generis* right), which is implemented by the **Copyright and Rights in Databases Regulations 1997**.

- Both computer programs and databases must be original in the sense of being the author's own **intellectual creation**.

- Computer programs:

  - copyright protects only the expression of a program, not the ideas underlying its interfaces;

  - there are protections to ensure that programs can be investigated and interoperable programs can be written.

- Databases:

  - copyright protects the 'selection and arrangement' of the database if it is original;

  - database right protects against substantial amounts of data being extracted from the database, provided **substantial investment** went into gathering the data.

Programs and databases described and distinguished

Computer programs contain instructions that cause a computer to do things with data. Some of the data stored on a computer will be in the form of a database, but some will not: a database is information recorded in an organized way so that individual items can be retrieved— disorganized data is not a database.

In the case of an electronic database, a computer program of some description will be needed to assist in accessing the data. Most suites of office productivity software include programs for creating and accessing databases, for example Access (part of the Microsoft Office Suite) and Base (part of the OpenOffice suite). The **Database Directive** (which came after the **Software Directive**) states that any programs necessary for accessing the data are to be dealt with under the **Software Directive** and are not part of a database.

Modern websites often comprise a database of content, software for adding and retrieving data from or to it (a database server), and software for communicating with users over the internet (a web server). So when you communicate with an online shop, social networking site, or discussion forum you are in fact adding data to and retrieving data from a database maintained by the site's owner.

Copyright in programs

Definitions

There is no definition of a computer program in the **Software Directive** or the **CDPA**. In both, a program is identified as a category of literary work that must be protected (s 3(1)(b) and (c)/Art 1.1). The US **Copyright Act of 1976** defines a program as:

> a set of statements or instructions to be used directly or indirectly in a computer in order to bring about a certain result.

While the Directive states that a computer program 'includes preparatory material for a computer program', the **CDPA** defines the program and preparatory work as separate types of literary work. The Act will be interpreted in light of the Directive, so provisions expressed to apply to 'computer programs' will apply also to the preparatory materials. Preparatory materials need dealing with otherwise authors could assert copyright in their preparatory materials that would circumvent program-specific rules.

In *Bezpečnostní softwarová asociace—Svaz softwarové ochrany v Ministerstvo kultury* [2011], the ECJ held that the appearance of the graphical user interface of a program was not part of the program because a functioning program could not be derived from it, but that it could be protected as a copyright work if it satisfied the **originality** test.

Originality and scope of protection

The **Software Directive** requires the **intellectual creation** test of originality to be applied to computer programs.

In addition, the Directive states in **Art 1.2** that

protection . . . shall apply to the expression in any form of a computer program

but that

ideas and principles which underlie any element of a computer program, including those which underlie its interfaces, are not protected.

This indicates a clear policy that copyright should not create monopolies over communications protocols and so on. This will have an effect on those acts of inexact copying that can infringe a program—see the discussion of infringement and the substantial part later in the chapter.

The **CDPA** does not exactly mirror this wording, but the courts nevertheless apply it following EU law principles—see the following section and Chapter 1 in relation to the impact of EU law.

Infringement of computer program copyright

The Directive prescribes the restricted acts in **Art 4**. These include temporary or permanent reproduction, translation, adaptation, and distribution to the public. The Act contains no special provisions for infringing acts, but the general infringing acts (that apply to all works—see Chapter 2) would cover those required by the Directive. Running a program will normally involve making a temporary copy in computer memory, and the Directive states expressly that, if that is so, it will infringe unless there is consent (**Art 4(a)**).

The High Court applied the Directive in *Navitaire Inc v easyJet* [2004]. It observed that it would be reluctant to hold infringement in any software case where there had been no copying at the level of lines of code, even if there was copying of more abstract elements. So, where the defendants had rewritten software to achieve the same purpose as the claimant's software, and copied many aspects of structure and communication, they had not taken a substantial part of the program.

In *SAS Institute v World Programming* [2012] (Chapter 2 Key Case), the ECJ interpreted Art 1 of the Directive as meaning that 'neither the functionality of a computer program nor the programming language and the format of data files used in a computer program . . . constitute a form of expression of that program'. So World were able to write software which interpreted the SAS language, meaning that programs written by SAS customers would run equally well when using the World software as they did when using the SAS software. This reflects a key underlying principle of the Directive.

Defences for programs

The Act in ss 50A–50C implements Arts 5 and 6 and provides defences for lawful users of programs to:

- make back-ups (note this defence does *not* apply to other works);
- decompile the program in order to create an independent program that can inter-operate (unless the necessary information to do so is available, for example in a published 'applications programming interface', known as an API);
- study the operation of the program to understand its underlying principles.

These defences cannot be overridden by contractual terms. There is also a general defence of doing anything that is necessary for the lawful use of the program provided it is not prohibited by agreement. In *SAS v World*, this was interpreted as meaning that World, which had an SAS licence, could run the software for the purpose of understanding its programming interface and not be in breach of its licence terms.

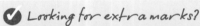 **Looking for extra marks?**

Although these defences apply to 'computer programs', they will be interpreted as applying also to preparatory material for computer programs so as to comply with the Directive.

Any of the general or specific defences that apply to literary works will apply also to preparatory materials and computer programs unless they are expressly excluded from the defence. An important exception is the 'temporary copies' defence in s 28A, which does not apply.

Protection of databases

Definition of a database

Databases are defined in the Database Directive and the CDPA in s 3A/Art 1 as:

> a collection of independent works, data or other materials which— (a) are arranged in a systematic or methodical way, and (b) are individually accessible by electronic or other means.

Not all tables and compilations that would amount to copyright works will be databases under this definition because of the requirements for systematic arrangement and individual accessibility, but suitably organized and accessible paper-based databases will, as will electronic databases. While music could be regarded as data about notes, and a digital image as data about pixel values, they are not databases as defined. The data are not independent—they are linked by the requirement collectively to represent a particular musical work or image.

Remember that something that does not meet the definition of a database may be protected by ordinary literary, dramatic, musical, or artistic copyright—perhaps as a 'table or compilation'.

The two ways a database may be protected

Anything falling within the definition may be protected:

- as a copyright work if it satisfies the test of originality and qualifies for protection: s 3(1)(d) provides that a database as defined is a type of literary work, as required by **Art 3**;
- under the *sui generis* right provided it satisfies the 'substantial investment' test and qualifies for protection (provided by the **Copyright and Rights in Databases Regulations 1997**, which implement the Directive).

A database may be protected under either one or both: they protect different things. See Figure 3.1.

Copyright protection of databases

Originality and existence of database copyright

CDPA, s 3A provides a definition of originality for databases to comply with the Directive—databases are entitled to copyright protection if:

by reason of the selection or arrangement of the contents of the database, the database represents the author's own intellectual creation.

Figure 3.1 Protection of databases

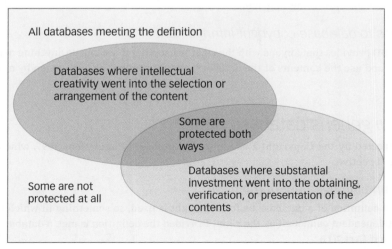

Protection of databases
****

The Directive also states that copyright protection in databases:

> shall not extend to their contents and shall be without prejudice to any rights subsisting in those contents themselves.

The UK High Court had held that the compilation of football league timetables involved intellectual creation, thus they are copyright databases following the EU test. (It had in earlier cases held that they satisfied the **skill and labour** test.) However, in *Football Dataco Ltd and others v Yahoo! UK Ltd and others* [2012], the ECJ held that creating a football league fixture list amounted to the creation of the data in the database, as distinct from its selection or arrangement, and therefore any intellectual creation involved did not count.

The football leagues have not always succeeded before the UK courts:

Football Dataco Ltd and others v Sportradar GmbH and another [2012] EWHC 1185 (Ch), [2012] 3 CMLR 18

FACTS: Dataco collected data at football matches such as passes, tackles, etc in a database.

HELD: This activity may have involved skill, eg in sorting out who scored in a goalmouth scramble, but it did not involve any intellectual creation in its selection or arrangement on the part of the data gatherers. The match data collected were the content of the database, so not protected by database copyright in any event.

Infringement of database copyright

To infringe copyright in a database, what is taken must reflect the intellectual creation *involved in the selection or arrangement* of the database (the originality). Thus, by taking the match data Sportradar did not take any of this, even if some intellectual creation had gone into the selection or arrangement.

Defences to database copyright infringement

Section 50D provides that anyone with the right to use a database can do anything necessary to access and use the contents of the database, and this cannot be overridden by a contractual term.

The *sui generis* database right

This is created by the Copyright and Rights in Databases Regulations 1997, which implement the Directive.

Nature and infringement of the right

The same definition of a database as for copyright is used, so something in which the data are not independent cannot enjoy the right. Provided the definition is met, a database enjoys protection if (Art 7(1)) there has been qualitatively and/or quantitatively a substantial investment in either the obtaining, verification or presentation of the contents . . . of that database.

The Directive protects against the

extraction or re-utilisation of the whole or of a substantial part, evaluated qualitatively and/or quantitatively of the contents of . . . that database

and states (Art 7(5)) that

The repeated and systematic extraction and/or re-utilisation of insubstantial parts of the contents of the database implying acts with conflict with a normal exploitation of that database or which unreasonably prejudice the legitimate interests of the maker of the database shall not be permitted.

This wording is not accurately reflected in the wording of the Regulations (reg 16), but the Directive will be followed.

In *British Horseracing Board Ltd v William Hill Organisation Ltd* [2005], the ECJ held that

- the 'substantial part' requirement referred to the investment in the database (ie where part has been taken, the investment in that part must be substantial for the taking to infringe);

- investment referred to 'resources used' and, thus, can include human labour and the use of expensive capital assets, as well as the paying out of money;

- only investment related to the obtaining, verification, or presentation of the contents counted (to the existence of the right and to its infringement).

The ECJ held that the lists of runners and riders for the races supervised by the British Horseracing Board (BHB) were *created* by it—and therefore the data were *not obtained* by it. It further held that any investment in the verification or presentation did not count as it was so connected with the creation of the data as to be inseparable from it. BHB thus failed in its attempt to enforce database right against betting companies that used its race data in their businesses.

A crucial matter in deciding whether database right exists is thus the question of whether the data is *obtained* or *created*.

The Court also held (*obiter*) that:

- extraction means taking data from the database and keeping copies of it (regardless of how the data were stored and whether the organization of the data was taken as well);

- to infringe under the 'systematic and repeated' ground, the insubstantial parts had to be kept so that, over time, a copy of a substantial part of the contents of the database came into existence.

Protection of databases

****

Re-utilization was addressed in *Innoweb*:

Innoweb BV v Wegener ICT Media BV (C-202/12) [2014] Bus LR 308

FACTS: Used-car sites including Innoweb compiled databases of cars for sale and a web 'front end' for visitors to search it. D provided a 'meta search engine' which automatically searched a number of such sites via their search facilities.

HELD: This amounted to re-utilizing Innoweb's database, a key reason being that the results were displayed in D's format with duplicate results grouped, rather than simply presenting the outputs of the websites searched.

That last point is important: not all meta search engines will infringe.

Defences to database right infringement and the 'lawful user'

Often databases become available to users as a result of a contract or licence—either entered into when media containing the database is purchased or in return for being granted access to a database via a network. The licensees in these cases are 'lawful users' (they did not have to hack their way in unlawfully). Some databases are available just by browsing the internet, in which case everyone is a lawful user.

Lawful users of a database that has been made available to the public may not be prevented from extracting or re-utilizing *insubstantial* parts of it (**Art 8/reg 19**)—that is, no contract whereby the data is made available can restrict the rights of the user, though a contract may grant the user more extensive rights.

As with copyright (see Chapter 2), the availability of a database via the internet does not imply freedom to do what you like with the data. Extracting or re-utilizing more than insubstantial parts will infringe. The content of most modern websites is contained in databases of materials in which database right may exist, so extensive downloading of material may involve infringement of database right in addition to infringement of copyright in the underlying material.

The Directive also *permits* further defences in **Art 9**, which may extend to the use of substantial parts of a database. The UK has implemented these in **reg 20**: fair dealing with a substantial part of the contents of a database is not an infringement if the part was extracted by a lawful user for the purpose of non-commercial teaching or research and the source is indicated.

Note: there is no general defence for private and non-commercial activities.

Qualification for, ownership of, and duration of the sui generis right

The first **owner** of database right is the person who made the investment in the gathering, etc of the data (see 'Nature and infringement of the right' earlier).

The right lasts for 15 years following the date of completion of the database, but if it is made available to the public within that time, 15 years from the date of making available (in both cases, the periods start on 1 January following the relevant date).

If a substantial change, evaluated qualitatively or quantitatively, is made to the contents of a database, resulting in a substantial new investment, then the 'database resulting from that investment' shall enjoy its own period of protection.

These provisions involve difficulty—in the case of databases that are constantly added to, presumably the right arises as soon as the investment goes over the 'substantial' level. But what does that mean? And what happens when a further substantial investment is made— does the new term apply just to the additions or to the whole database? These issues were not considered by the ECJ in *BHB* (though they were by the Advocate-General) and so remain open.

As for qualification, people who are nationals of or resident in the EU and companies incorporated in an EU state or that have their central administration or place of business there, qualify. There are provisions to extend this to territories that offer reciprocal protection— but there are few such territories.

Criticism and discussion of database protection

Database right is named *sui generis* because it is a right that bears no similarity to any previously existing IP right. Prior to the Directive, there was considerable debate in the UK as to how the law would protect directories and such like. The US case of *Feist v Rural Telephone* is often used for comparison.

Feist Publications Inc v Rural Telephone Service Co 499 US 340 (1991)

FACTS: Copyright was asserted in a telephone directory.

HELD: US copyright does not protect information, but it can protect collections of information if creativity is exercised. The standard of creativity is extremely low; there need only be a 'spark' or 'minimal degree' of creativity. Rural's directory of all its subscribers involved no creativity at all. The time and money spent collecting the data were not relevant.

It is not clear that the same result would have followed in a similar UK case following the 'skill and labour' originality test. The Directive has dealt with the copyright issue—the requirement for selection and arrangement makes asserting copyright in databases that are intended to be comprehensive difficult. But many have criticized database right as being an unnecessary intervention.

Key cases

✳✳✳✳✳✳✳✳✳✳

Case	Facts	Principle
Bezpečnostní softwarová asociace—Svaz softwarové ochrany v Ministerstvo kultury [2011] ECDR 3 (ECJ)	Czech software houses alleged that by transmitting TV programmes that showed the screens of computers displaying the graphical user interfaces (GUIs) of their programs, copyright in the programs was being infringed.	The GUIs were not part of the computer programs as an operable program could not be derived from them, but they would be entitled to protection as copyright works subject to the requirement for originality. GUIs are not communicated to the public by broadcasting their images because their essential element (communication with the computer) is not accessible to the viewer of the broadcast.
Navitaire Inc v easyJet (No 3) [2004] EWHC 1725 (Ch)	easyJet had procured software to replace Navitaire's product, which enabled communication with standard booking software used by travel agents. It therefore reproduced those aspects of the Navitaire software which enabled that to occur.	It was the wording and interpretation of the Directive that governed the law, not that of the Act (to the extent the Act differed). The layouts of GUI screens were capable of being artistic works and thus not subject to the Directive. A collection of commands was not a computer program and was not a protectable literary work unless it was original. Obvious steps to implement a procedure in code could not amount to a substantial part of a computer program.
Football Dataco Ltd and others v Yahoo! UK Ltd and others (C-604/10) [2012] 2 CMLR 24	The claimants claimed copyright in fixture lists for English and Scottish league football. The defendants needed to copy them to offer gambling products ('football pools') to their customers. The arrangement of a season's matches was not done automatically; it took into account the complex interaction of a number of factors, which required skill and labour.	Database copyright did not protect the contents of a database (in this case, the dates and teams of the games). For copyright to exist, therefore, there needed to be intellectual creation in the selection or arrangement of the data over and above what was involved in the process of fixing the match teams, dates, and times.

Case	Facts	Principle
British Horseracing Board Ltd v William Hill Organisation Ltd (C-203/02) [2005] 1 CMLR 15	BHB can allow or refuse entry to races and has statutory duties in relation to the organization of horseracing. The defendants needed to reproduce lists of runners and riders, prepared by BHB, in order to offer gambling services. The ECJ held that the information in the lists was not obtained by BHB; rather, it was created by it.	Database right requires investment, which must be in the obtaining, verification, or presentation of the contents of the database. Investment in creating the data that goes into the database does not count. A substantial part of a database (for the purposes of infringement) is data the obtaining, etc of which required a substantial investment.

💬 Key debates

Topic	Was the introduction of database right worth it?
Author	J H Reichman and Pamela Samuelson
Standpoint	Argue that the EU approach to protecting databases is restrictive and unnecessary.
Source	'Intellectual Property Rights in Data' (1997) 50 Vanderbilt L Rev 52–166

Author	European Commission
Standpoint	Adopts a neutral stance on the future of database right, offering the options to scrap it, continue it as it is, or change it.
Source	'First evaluation of Directive 96/9/EC on the legal protection of Databases', 12 December 2005

Author	Estelle Derclaye
Standpoint	A thorough review of the position.
Source	'Intellectual Property Rights on Information and Market Power—Comparing European and American Protection of Databases' (2007) 38(3) IIC 275–298 (on Westlaw)

? Exam question

Problem question

Gary has for many years been a supporter of Southern League football club Basingstoke Warriors FC. Gary keeps a diary of all the matches he has attended, including match statistics and his

Exam question

✱✱✱✱✱✱✱✱✱✱

impressions of the game. He obtains the match statistics from the 'matchinfo.com' website, which is maintained by the League using data from their team of match reporters. Gary makes his diaries available to all supporters via a website. To do this, Gary divided the information in his diary into categories that he chose, such as 'pies', 'chants', 'PA announcements', and so on. He created the website using standard software, with which he made a database to hold the information and a user-friendly 'front-end', by which browsers could access the information for any match of their choosing.

What intellectual property rights will Gary have as a result of his diary and website, and is he infringing any of the League's rights by taking information from matchinfo.com?

See the Outline Answers section in the end matter for help with this question.

#4
Moral rights

Key facts

There are two quite different types of rights labelled as 'moral rights' in the **Copyright, Designs and Patents Act 1988 (CDPA)**:

- Rights for authors, which implement the provisions of the **Berne Convention, Art 6 bis** ('the Berne rights'):

    - to be identified as author of a copyright literary, dramatic or musical **work** or director of a film, provided it has first been asserted;

    - not to have their copyright work subjected to **derogatory treatment**—that is, an alteration to the work that has an effect on the author's honour or reputation.

    These two rights are referred to as the rights of paternity and integrity, respectively.

- Other rights of individuals, not necessarily authors:

    - the right not to be falsely **attributed** as author of a literary, dramatic, musical, or artistic work or as director of a film;

    - a right of privacy in privately commissioned *copyright* photographs and films that applies even if the commissioner is not the copyright **owner**.

(These two rights are not universally known as 'moral rights' outside the UK.)

Introduction

The Berne rights protect the relationship between authors and their works other than rights to exploit them commercially (those are protected by copyright and known as the author's 'economic rights'). Thus, they cannot be assigned, and may be enforced even after the author has assigned or licensed their economic rights and even against the owner or licensee. The rights last as long as copyright does and pass to the author's beneficiaries after the author's death.

Different countries have implemented the Berne rights in different ways. The UK has implemented them in a way that favours the rights of the owner over those of the author, and this has been criticized. Civil law countries have implemented the rights in a way that gives authors much more power over their works.

This difference reflects the different theoretical basis of copyright protection in different countries. In civil law countries, where the **authors' rights** approach holds sway, moral rights have existed for as long as copyright. The **skill and labour** and 'sweat of the brow' approach in common law countries is less compatible with the idea of moral rights.

The Berne rights did not become specifically implemented in UK law until the CDPA in 1988. **Article 6 bis** of Berne says:

> (1) Independently of the author's economic rights, and even after the transfer of the said rights, the author shall have the right to claim authorship of the work and to object to any distortion, mutilation or other modification of, or other derogatory action in relation to, the said work, which would be prejudicial to his honor or reputation.

Other common law jurisdictions, such as the United States and Australia, have also only introduced the Berne rights relatively recently. (The **TRIPs Agreement, Art 9** requires compliance with the **Berne Convention** generally, but **Art 6 bis** is expressly excluded from this.)

The other rights are not required by Berne and include other legal considerations, though they relate also to copyright. They are included in the Act under the chapter heading 'Moral Rights', so are dealt with here.

Moral rights in detail

The right to be attributed as author

Structure of the provisions

The Act constructs the right in the following way—each of these aspects will be dealt with in turn:

- the basic right to be attributed as author (s 77(1));
- occasions on which attribution must be made (s 77(2)–(6));
- how the attribution must be made (s 77(7)–(9));
- the need for the right to be asserted, and methods by which it may be asserted (s 78);

- exclusions (s 79)—these include exclusions of works from the right and exclusions relating to particular uses of works.

The basic right (s 77(1))

The key words in the Act are 'the right to be attributed as author', which is given to authors of all authorial works and directors of films, provided UK copyright exists in them (thus they must be qualifying works—see Chapter 2). The right lasts as long as copyright in the work.

In *Sawkins v Hyperion Records* [2005], it was held that for there to be an attribution as author there must be a clear statement that the author was indeed the author of the work. So when Dr Sawkins was thanked for his 'preparation of performance materials for this recording', that was not sufficient.

Occasions when there must be an attribution (s 77(2)–(6))

There are different provisions for different types of work. You will need to refer to your statute book when dealing with a particular situation—note particularly the concept of 'commercial publication' defined in s 175. Broadly speaking:

- issuing copies of a work to the public, and
- performing it in or communicating or exhibiting it to the public

are likely to trigger the right. In the case of artistic works, exhibition of the work triggers the rights, as does the issue to the public of graphic works depicting, or photographs of, buildings, works of artistic craftsmanship, or sculptures. See Chapter 2 for the statutory definitions of 'performing' and 'communicating to the public'. There are many exceptions to this basic principle; only the important ones are described here.

Important exceptions to the need for attribution

The so-called 'disc jockey exception' applies to *musical works and lyrics*. The right is not triggered by broadcasting and is only triggered by making available electronically in a commercial setting.

Acts of *private* copying and distribution that might amount to infringement of copyright do not trigger the right. Private sharing, uploading, and downloading of music files are examples of this.

In the case of *buildings*, the architect must be identified when the building is built, but in the case of multiple buildings made to the same design, only on the first one made.

Manner of attribution (s 77(7)–(9))

The general requirement is that the identification must be 'clear and reasonably prominent'. There is more detailed guidance in the Act for specific situations:

- In the case of commercial publication or issuing, the attribution must be contained on the copies published or issued. Where this is 'not appropriate', the attribution should be 'in some other manner likely to bring [the author's] identity to the notice of a person acquiring a copy'.

- In the case of buildings, the attribution must be 'visible to persons entering or approaching the building'.

- In other cases the attribution must be such as is 'likely to bring [the author's] identity to the attention of a person seeing or hearing the performance, exhibition, showing or communication to the public'.

The need for the right to be asserted (s 78)

The requirement for assertion is often cited by critics of the way the Berne rights have been implemented by the **CDPA**. In addition to assertion being a requirement for the right to exist, *delay in asserting* the right can affect any remedy that might be granted.

Assertion must be by one of the means set out in s 78 to be effective. These are:

- *in an assignment or licence of the copyright*—this will bind anyone obtaining rights in relation to the work pursuant to that assignment or licence;

- *by 'an instrument in writing signed by the author'* (ie a signed document)—this will bind anyone who has notice of the instrument;

- *in relation to the public exhibition of artistic works*—the author may assert their rights:

    - by putting their name on the original or an authorized copy, in which case anyone responsible for exhibiting the original or that copy is bound by the assertion; or

    - in writing in a licence permitting the public exhibition of the work, in which case anyone exhibiting the work pursuant to that permission is bound (even if they do not have notice of the assertion in the licence).

✅ Looking for extra marks?

In appropriate cases you should point out the dubious treaty basis for the need for assertion of the right to be identified as author. **Article 6 bis of the Berne Convention** is as follows:

(1) Independently of the author's economic rights, and even after the transfer of the said rights, the author shall have the right to claim authorship of the work and . . .

The argument for the UK requirement that the right be asserted is based on the words 'to claim'. However, that is an extreme interpretation of the wording. It is difficult to see any justification for such strict requirements other than to make life as easy as possible for exploiters of works and as difficult as possible for authors, and other countries have not interpreted Berne in this way.

Exclusions (s 79)

The other main aspect of the statutory provisions that is often criticized is the number and scope of the exclusions from the right.

Works for which the right is excluded completely

Some works are excluded from the requirement in all circumstances:

- **computer programs** (see Chapter 3);
- designs of typefaces (these will be artistic works);
- computer-generated works (see Chapter 2—such works are likely to be rare, if they exist at all);
- works created for the purpose of reporting current events (see Chapter 2 for the meaning of this, which is used in relation to defences to copyright infringement).

People for whom the right is excluded

In other cases, some categories of people can ignore the right:

- Where the author's employer was the first owner (see Chapter 2 on ownership), the right does not apply to acts carried out with the authority of the copyright owner (ie acts of the employer or the employer's licensees, or any subsequent owners of copyright or their licensees).
- Where an LDMA work is published in a newspaper, magazine, or similar periodical, or work of collective reference, the right does not apply if the work was created for the publication or included in it with the author's consent (note that this exclusion does not apply to films).

Employees will still have their right in relation to activities not covered by these exclusions.

Exclusions where defences to copyright infringement apply (s 79(4))

In some (but not all) situations, if a defence to copyright infringement can be made out (see Chapter 2), there is also a defence to the requirement to identify the author. The important defences are:

- s 30 (fair dealing for criticism and review, quotation, and reporting)—no requirement to identify the author in the case of reporting current events by means of a sound recording, film, or broadcast, but there is in other cases where the defence applies;
- s 31 (incidental inclusion)—no requirement to identify the author where the defence applies;
- ss 51 (use of design documents and models)—no requirement to identify the author where the defence applies.

The situation of reporting current events needs to be looked at in conjunction with the exclusion of works created for that purpose in s 79(5) (see 'Works for which the right is excluded completely', discussed earlier).

Moral rights in detail

✳✳✳✳✳✳✳✳✳✳

There is no exclusion in cases where the defences of criticism and review, parody or quotation are relied on. There is also no exclusion in relation to the defence of research or private study—though it is unlikely that the need to identify the author would arise in such situations.

You should consult your statute book for a full list of the copyright defences where the right to be attributed is also affected.

The right to object to derogatory treatment of a work

The basic right is set out in s 80:

(1) The author of a copyright literary, dramatic, musical or artistic work, and the director of a copyright film, has the right in the circumstances mentioned in this section not to have his work subjected to derogatory treatment.

(2) For the purposes of this section—

(a) 'treatment' of a work means any addition to, deletion from or alteration to or adaptation of the work, other than—

(i) a translation of a literary or dramatic work, or

(ii) an arrangement or transcription of a musical work involving no more than a change of key or register;

and

(b) the treatment of a work is derogatory if it amounts to distortion or mutilation of the work or is otherwise prejudicial to the honour or reputation of the author or director;

As with the right to be attributed as author, the right only exists in relation to works qualifying for UK copyright and only lasts as long as the copyright.

The definition of 'derogatory treatment'

A number of important issues of interpretation and doctrine arise from the wording of s 80:

• what activities do and do not amount to a 'treatment';

• the effect of the exclusions of translations, etc from the definition of a treatment;

• the meaning of 'derogatory treatment';

• what amounts to damage to an author's reputation.

Activities amounting to a 'treatment'

All the activities mentioned require some change to the work. This is often summarized as a requirement that the 'internal structure' of the work is changed. This interpretation was confirmed in the case of *Pasterfield v Denham [1999]*, where changes to the text surrounding a graphic work were ignored by the court in considering whether the work had been treated in a derogatory manner.

Harrison v Harrison [2010] FSR 25

FACTS: A subsequent edition of a book was written without the consent of the original author.

HELD (*obiter*): Anything that could result in damage to reputation could be a 'treatment'; as a previously unpublished author, Harrison arguably had no reputation and so there could be no derogatory treatment.

Example

Hanging pictures in an exhibition alongside obscene or extremist material cannot be a derogatory treatment, though it might have an effect on the artist's reputation.

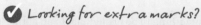 **Looking for extra marks?**

The use of the concept of a 'treatment' here can be contrasted with the wording of **Art 6 bis of the Berne Convention**, which talks of derogatory actions *in relation to* the work. The Berne wording would encompass activities surrounding the work that did not result in any alteration to its internal structure, and in many countries such activity could potentially be derogatory treatment.

The things that are excluded from being a 'treatment'

Even if the activities complained of meet the definition of a 'treatment', the exclusions in s 80(2)(a)(i) and (ii) need to be considered. Taking s 80(2)(b)(ii) first, the wording makes it clear that any change to the musical work that goes beyond a change of key or register will be considered a 'treatment'. But in relation to s 80(2)(b)(i), two interpretations are possible:

- provided the work is translated, no changes to it amount to a 'treatment'; or
- changes to the work that arise from the translation will not amount to 'treatment' but changes that are not related to the act of translating will be considered 'treatments'.

The second interpretation is more favourable to original authors so, for example, large-scale changes of plot in a translation would not fall within the exclusion.

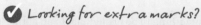 **Looking for extra marks?**

The second interpretation can be supported by considering Parliament's intention. Presumably the intention was to provide certainty for translators, while implementing the **Berne Convention**. The second interpretation is the more balanced approach to this. The **Berne Convention** was used as an interpretative aid in *Pasterfield*—see 'The meaning of "derogatory"' below, which supports this interpretative approach.

Moral rights in detail
✱✱✱✱✱✱✱✱✱✱

The meaning of 'derogatory'

In *Pasterfield*, the court interpreted the wording of s 80(2)(b) as a whole and took into account the presumed intention of Parliament to implement the terms of the **Berne Convention**. This led the court to the conclusion that distortions and mutilations are only actionable if they are prejudicial to the honour or reputation of the author. The observation in *Harrison* (discussed earlier) that an author must have built up a reputation as an author before being able to sue is, however, questionable.

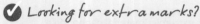

Looking for extra marks?

Do not, therefore, discuss in detail the meaning of the words 'distort' or 'mutilate' in your essays and answers, because nothing hangs on the precise interpretation of those words. The words that need careful consideration are 'prejudicial to his honour or reputation'.

The difficult question is thus, what does it mean for something to be prejudicial to an author's honour or reputation?

Prejudice to the *author's* honour or reputation

In *Confetti Records v Warner Music UK Ltd [2003]*, it was held that evidence of an author's actual reputation might be needed, and that a genuine feeling of upset on the part of the author was required *in addition to* that feeling of upset being objectively reasonable.

Looking for extra marks?

The cases leave a number of questions open, such as how and whether to distinguish an author's personal reputation (as in defamation) from their artistic reputation, how to establish what the artistic reputation is (from fans, for example, or from expert critics), and how that might be prejudiced (what about artists who cultivate a 'bad boy' image?). In your essays and answers, you should explore possible further interpretations of the law while making it clear when you are doing so.

Acts that infringe the right

Section 80 goes on to set out the acts that, committed in relation to a derogatory treatment, infringe the right. These encompass most acts of issuing copies, performing in, and communicating to the public a derogatory treatment. Acts done privately do not infringe the right—but if the derogatory treatment is communicated to the public (eg by uploading to a video-sharing internet site), that will be an infringement, even if it is done in a personal capacity.

Exclusions from the right to object to derogatory treatment

These are contained in s 81, and as with the exclusions from the right to be attributed as author, are a subject of criticism because of their breadth:

- The right does not apply to computer programs, computer-generated works, and works made for the purposes of reporting current events.
- Where an LDMA work is published in a newspaper, magazine, or similar periodical, or an encyclopaedia, dictionary, yearbook, or other collective work of reference, the right does not apply if the work was created for the publication or included in it with the author's consent (note that this exclusion does not apply to films).

There is an exception in relation to employee's works, but it is only partial: if the employee has been identified in relation to the work, then the right does apply, though it is not infringed if there is 'a sufficient disclaimer'.

Unlike the right to be identified as author, the right to object to derogatory treatment is not excluded in any situations in which the main defences to copyright infringement (the fair dealing defences, incidental inclusion, etc) apply. Notably, even where the defence of parody, etc applies, that is no defence to derogatory treatment.

The right not to be falsely attributed as author

Section 84 is as follows:

(1) A person has the right in the circumstances mentioned in this section—

   (a) not to have a literary, dramatic, musical or artistic work falsely attributed to him as author, and

   (b) not to have a film falsely attributed to him as director;

A 'work' means anything satisfying the definitions contained in CDPA, ss 1–4, regardless of whether or not it is original, or if copyright subsists in it. All individuals (ie natural people, not corporations) have the right.

In *Noah v Shuba* [1991], the court held that making alterations without the consent of the author infringed the right where the author of the whole work was indicated in the normal way, because the alterations amounted to a separate 'work'.

Revision tip

The finding in *Noah v Shuba* is consistent with the law on copyright works and authorship—re-read Chapter 2 if it is not clear to you that this is so.

In *Clark v Associated Newspapers* [1991], the court held that the test of what amounted to an attribution as author was functional—would a substantial number of readers of the publication think the wrong person was the author? The court took into account the nature of the work and how carefully it was read in deciding this—here evening newspapers are not read with great care, often on public transport, and over the shoulder of another reader.

Note: Clark sued in passing-off as well—see Chapter 9.

Ghostwriters

Ghostwriters are professional writers who write books or autobiographies that are then published as if written by someone else. Potentially, the actual writer's right to be identified as author is engaged, as well as the pretend author's right not to be falsely attributed.

Moore v News of the World [1972] 1 QB 441

FACTS: A newspaper attributed quotes to an interviewee, though she had not uttered those words.

HELD: This amounted to false attribution of those words to the interviewee.
    If all parties consent to the arrangements, for example in a publishing contract, there is no problem with this type of arrangement.

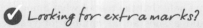

Revision tip

It is easy to confuse this right with the right of paternity and apply cases from one right to the other on the question of attribution. This is incorrect. What might fool enough people to be an attribution for the purposes of s 84 (as in the *Clark* case) may not be sufficiently certain to satisfy the requirement to give an attribution in s 77 (as in the *Sawkins* case). Take care to keep the concepts and cases separate.

The right of privacy in some photographs and films

Section 85 gives people who have commissioned photographs and films, in which copyright subsists, for 'private and domestic purposes' the right not to have the work issued, exhibited, shown, or communicated to the public. This right only lasts as long as copyright in the work. (Remember, a commissioned photographer will not be an employee, so the commissioner will not automatically own copyright—see Chapter 2.)

✅ *Looking for extra marks?*

Where this right may be in issue, consider alternative remedies. Could it be argued that the commissioning contract contained express or implied terms as to ownership or privacy?

➡ But note also that professional photographers typically expressly retain copyright in their standard terms. Will the commissioner be able to argue a breach of the privacy branch of the law of confidence (see Chapter 6)?

Remedies for breach of moral rights

The rights are all actionable as breaches of statutory duty (**CDPA, s 103**). Damages for infringement and injunctions to restrain anticipated or further infringement are available in the usual way, but there are no provisions for additional damages. In relation to the right to object to derogatory treatment, **s 103** gives the court power (effectively) to allow the infringer to continue provided a suitable disclaimer is given if it thinks that would be an adequate remedy.

Contract, consent, and waiver of the rights

Section 87 provides that it is not an infringement of any of the rights to do things with consent. It also provides for waiver of the rights, in relation to a specific work or works generally (including future works). So, for example, a songwriter could waive their rights in future works in a recording or publishing contract and a recording artist could consent to be attributed as co-writer of the songs they perform, even if they took no part in their creation.

None of the rights can be assigned: on the death of an author, the Berne rights pass to the author's estate.

Interaction between the moral rights and copyright

Whenever a work is misused in some way, there is the possibility of both copyright infringement and infringement of moral rights. In the case of inexact copying, it is unlikely that the original author will be identified, and possible that the changes amount to a derogatory treatment—so if the copyright claim can be made out (bearing in mind the substantial part test), infringement of moral rights may also be present. If the copyist does identify the author in the case of inexact copying, it may be a case of false attribution (*Noah*).

Two of the cases in this chapter (*Pasterfield* and *Confetti Records*) are in fact cases where a copyright claim was not possible for contractual reasons, and moral rights were relied on as a substitute to achieve a commercial objective. Both cases failed. It is in situations where the author no longer holds the economic rights and has a *genuine* grievance that moral rights are likely to provide a useful remedy.

Key cases

****

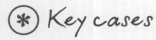

Case	Facts	Principle
Attribution as author		
Sawkins v Hyperion Records [2005] RPC 32	On a music CD, Dr Sawkins was merely thanked for his contribution, though in fact he was the author.	It is not enough to name the author; this must be done is such a way as to indicate clearly their role as an author.
Right to object to derogatory treatment		
Tidy v Trustees of Natural History Museum [1996] EIPR D-86	Cartoons drawn as posters were reproduced in postcard size and the author (a famous cartoonist) objected. His claim failed.	For derogatory treatment, what matters is public perception, which must be objectively reasonable. The author's genuine sense of upset is not sufficient.
Pasterfield v Denham [1999] FSR 168	A design consultancy had prepared artwork for a brochure and assigned copyright to the client. The client later produced an updated version, altering the text surrounding the graphics and altering the graphics slightly, though the changes would only be noticeable on a close examination. The claim failed.	The provisions of **Art 6 bis of the Berne Convention** can be used as an aid to interpretation of **CDPA, s 80**. Only alterations to the work itself can be treatments; additions, etc around the work (such as the text changes) are not treatments. For a treatment to be derogatory it must prejudice the honour or reputation of the author. *Tidy* was approved in relation to the test for prejudice to honour and reputation; it was the author's reputation *as an artist* that mattered.
Confetti Records v Warner Music UK Ltd [2003] EWHC 1274 (Ch), [2003] EMLR 35	A rap piece called 'Burnin' was adapted. The original lyrics consisted of the word 'burning' repeated periodically with a few other simple phrases. The defendants added their own words (many of which appeared to use obscure slang) on top of this. The claimants (the copyright owners and original author) alleged that the added words amounted to a derogatory treatment and suggested that they referred to illegal activity. No evidence was presented of the slang meaning of the words, of the author's reputation, or of his feelings about the adaptation.	(a) If the author cannot show they genuinely feel that their honour or reputation has been prejudiced, the court will not find that it has been. (b) Authors may have to set out what they say the message given about them by the treatment is in order to show that it is derogatory. (c) Even if the author is upset, there must, on an objective view, be damage to their reputation (ie the author's hurt feelings are a necessary but not sufficient condition). And (d) Evidence of the author's actual reputation may be required in order to establish (c).

Case	Facts	Principle
Right not to be falsely attributed as author or director		
Noah v Shuba [1991] FSR 14	The defendants made small material alterations to a work by Dr Noah and published it. The court found that the alterations amounted to a work and that Dr Noah had been falsely attributed as its author.	Following copyright principles, alterations or additions to a work are separate works. It is a breach of the **s 84** right when the whole altered work, including the alterations, is attributed to the author without his consent and with no indication that it has been altered.
Clarke v Associated Newspapers [1991] FSR 14	An evening newspaper column was entitled 'Alan Clark's Secret Political Diaries', though that was followed by a (less prominent) statement, which made it clear that the column was a spoof. The court found that evening papers are often not read with great care. The case on false attribution succeeded.	The relevant question is 'Would a substantial number of readers of the work think the claimant is the author?' In deciding this, the court should take into account the nature of the work and how it is normally read.

🔟 *Key debates*

Topic	Has the UK implemented the provisions of Art 6 bis effectively, and if not should they be strengthened?
Author	Gerald Dworkin
Standpoint	Acknowledges the difficulties in bringing authors' rights concepts into the common law legal tradition and argues that **Art 6 bis** does not sufficiently recognize the need to balance the rights of authors and exploiters of works.
Source	'The Moral Right of the Author: Moral Rights and the Common Law Countries' (1994–1995) 19 VLA J L & Arts 229–268.

Author	Irini Stamatoudi
Standpoint	Argues in favour of providing stronger protection for authors in the area of moral rights so that the non-economic rights of authors are fully recognized.
Source	'Moral Rights of Authors in England: The Missing Emphasis on the Role of Creators' [1997] 4 IPQ 447–513

Exam questions

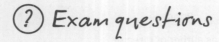
(?) Exam questions

Problem question

Janice was a popular comedian whose act included satirical songs reflecting her political views. She died in 2010. One of her popular songs was 'Mice and Soup', which made fun of climate-change sceptics. The song's tune was that of a popular standard, which Janice had obtained permission to use; the lyrics were written by Janice. When Janice died, all her assets (including copyright in her work) were sold to raise money for charity, in accordance with her wishes. Recently, Janice's widower Mike noticed on yourvid.com (a video-sharing website based in England) a song called 'Mice and Men', which was to the same tune as 'Mice and Soup' and with similar words, but with the lyrics altered in key areas to present a different message. The video shows Geraldine, who is a prominent anti-abortion campaigner, singing the song and Geraldine uploaded it. It does not mention Janice. Mike is upset at this, as the song presents an anti-abortion message, whereas Janice had been a strong supporter of a woman's right to choose an abortion.

What can Mike do about this?

See the Outline Answers section in the end matter for help with this question.

Essay question

The **Copyright Designs and Patents Act 1988**, as it has been interpreted by the courts, does not adequately implement the moral rights contained in **Article 6 bis of the Berne Convention**.

Discuss.

@ Online Resource Centre

To see an outline answer to this question visit www.oup.com/lawrevision/

#5

Performers' rights

Key facts

Performers' rights (correctly known as 'rights in performances') give musicians, singers, actors, dancers, and variety performers rights to prevent or give permission for:

- the recording or broadcasting of their live performances;

- subsequent commercial exploitation of those recordings, for example by the production and distribution of copies and by subsequent broadcasting and making available via the internet.

Performers' rights and copyright in sound recordings are closely related: the producer of the sound recording will be the person who arranges for the performers to perform, and will ensure that the performers give all the necessary permissions in their contracts to enable the sound recording to be exploited (see Figure 5.1).

Overview, history, and theory

Figure 5.1 Musical performers and other rights

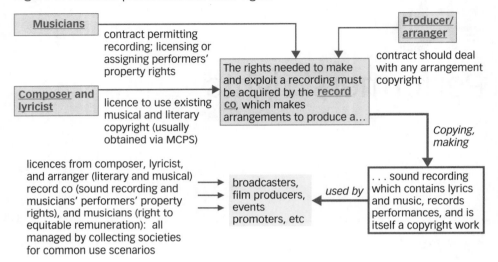

Overview, history, and theory

Performers' rights arose as a result of the development of sound recording technology, which meant that it was not necessary to hire the services of a performer in order to enjoy their performance. In the UK, the Performers' Protection Acts made it a criminal offence to record a performance without the consent of the performer. Subsequent case-law held that a civil action for breach of statutory duty was available to performers where the criminal offence had been committed.

The Copyright, Designs and Patents Act 1988 (CDPA) dealt with performers' rights in the same way, creating a criminal offence and giving performers a civil right of action. However, in 1996 it was amended to implement EU Directive 92/100/EEC on rental right and lending right (now codified in Directive 2006/115/EC on rental right and lending right).

Performers' rights are harmonized internationally by the Rome Convention for the Protection of Performers, Producers of Sound Recordings and Broadcasting Organizations, and by the WIPO Performances and Phonograms Treaty. While most developed countries recognize performers' rights, the international scope of these conventions is not as broad as that of the Berne Convention.

The main basis for having performers' rights is to give performers more control over the exploitation of their performances, thereby giving them bargaining power against record-ers and broadcasters. Although performers' property rights make performers' rights appear similar to copyright, there is an important difference: performers' rights do not protect the artistic or creative input of the performer—they provide no protection against imitation.

How performers' rights arise

Whenever a 'performance' as defined in the Act is made in qualifying circumstances, rights in the performance will arise and will belong to the performer. In addition, any person having exclusive recording rights in relation to the performer (eg a musical performer's record company) will acquire certain rights.

Experience Hendrix LLC v Purple Haze Records Ltd [2005] EWHC 249 (Ch), [2005] EMLR 18

HELD: Rights belong individually to each performer, so permission must be obtained from each band member if a recording of a performance by a band is to be exploited.

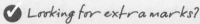 **Looking for extra marks?**

A separate performer's right will arise each time the performer goes on stage (assuming qualifying circumstances). It is the performance that is protected, not the act or routine. Always try to be as specific as you can about which performance gave rise to the right you are discussing. In the case of a suspected infringement, this will be the performance that is likely to have been copied or broadcast.

The definition of 'performance'

Section 180 defines a performance as being:

(a) a dramatic performance (which includes dance and mime),

(b) a musical performance,

(c) a reading or recitation of a literary work, or

(d) a performance of a variety act or any similar presentation,

which is, or so far as it is, a live performance given by one or more individuals; . . .

For categories (a), (b), and (c) an underlying work (literary, dramatic, or musical) must arguably exist. But note that the underlying work does not need to be a copyright work. It does not need to be original, and does not need to qualify for copyright protection. Recitations of medieval literature and stand-up comedy involving old jokes will amount to recitations or performances of works. Whenever a script is read from, there will be a performance—so newsreaders and television presenters will probably be performers. A chat-show host may be (if the questions are prepared), although a guest on their sofa probably will not be.

Category (d) would include activities where there is no underlying copyright work but which are done for entertainment purposes—this might apply, for example, to animal training acts, card tricks, feats of memory, and so on.

The rights given to performers

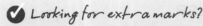

> ### ✅ Looking for extra marks?
>
> In many cases, an underlying dramatic work will be present in entertainment acts since rehearsed movements and sequences of events will be involved (see Chapter 2). This can be important: if a performer claims their act is being copied by another live performer, performers' rights will be of no assistance, but it might be possible to assert literary or dramatic copyright in the content of the act. Always consider the copyright (and possibly moral rights) position as well as the performers' rights position.

Qualifying performances

The scheme for qualification follows that for copyright—a performance may qualify:

- because it was made in a qualifying country; or
- because it was made by an individual who was at the time a citizen or subject of, or a resident in, a qualifying country (**CDPA, s 206**).

A 'qualifying country' means the UK, another EU state, or any other country designated by an Order in Council under **s 208**, which requires that for a country to be designated it must be a party to a convention regarding performers' rights or which offers reciprocal protection for performers. Most developed countries are designated under this provision, but many countries that are qualifying countries for the purposes of authorial copyright (because they are signatories to the **Berne Convention**) do not recognize performers' rights. For a complete list, consult the statutory instrument made under s 208— currently the **Copyright and Performances (Application to Other Countries) Order 2016** (**SI 2016/1219**).

The rights given to performers

The 1996 amendments introduced harmonized 'performers' property rights', required by the Rental and Lending Rights Directive, covering the exploitation of recordings of performances. The Act deals with the recording and broadcasting of live performances as 'non-property rights'. The distinction between the two types of right is discussed in 'Exploitation of performers' rights' later in the chapter.

Table 5.1 lists the key features of the rights, in the order they are likely to arise in the course of the exploitation of a recording of a performance, where:

- recording' means recording by a film or sound recording;
- references to a performance or recording of a performance include the whole or a substantial part of a performance.

Table 5.1 The main activities requiring the consent of the performer

Property rights	Non-property rights	Description
	s 182	Recording or broadcasting a live performance, recording a live broadcast.
s 182A		Making a copy of a recording (including transient copies and copies of copies) of a performance.
s 182B		Issuing copies to the public (known as the 'distribution right'). See Chapter 2. 'Issuing' means the first putting on sale of a copy within the EEA.
s 182C		Rental or lending of copies to the public.
s 182CA		Making copies available to the public. The wording is the same as that for making available rights under **CDPA, s 20. See Chapter 2: downloading or streaming must be at a time chosen by the user (otherwise it is 'broadcasting' and will infringe under s 183).**
	s 183	Showing or playing in public, or communicating to the public by means of a recording, knowing or having reason to believe that the recording was made without the performer's consent. 'Communicating to the public' has the same meaning as in **CDPA, s 20**.
	s 184	Importing (other than for private and domestic use), or selling, letting for hire, offering, or exposing for sale or hire, or distributing in the course of business an 'illicit recording' of the performance, knowing or having reason to believe it is an illicit recording.

Revision tip

Read the sections from your statute book and make sure that you can apply the correct right or rights to a particular situation, and do not confuse the rights performers have with the rights of record companies (see 'Rights of record companies—recording rights' later in this chapter).

Infringement under ss 183 and 184

Under both ss 183 and 184, the mental element will presumably be interpreted as it is for **secondary infringement** of copyright—see Chapter 2.

The rights given to performers
✳✳✳✳✳✳✳✳✳✳

'Illicit recording' in s 184 is defined in s 197 as a recording made, otherwise than for private purposes, without the consent of the performer. Into this definition the definition of 'recording' in s 180 needs to be plugged:

'recording', in relation to a performance, means a film or sound recording—

(a) made directly from the live performance,

(b) made from a broadcast of the performance, or

(c) made, directly or indirectly, from another recording of the performance.

Thus, every time a recording of a performance is copied, a further 'recording' is made, and if that further recording is made without consent, it is an illicit recording.

Bassey and another v Icon Entertainment Plc and another [1995] EMLR 596

HELD: Even if there is consent to the original recording ('fixation') of the performance, unless there is also consent to the making of copies of the recording, the copies will be illicit recordings and dealings in them may infringe under s 184.

These provisions can be viewed as secondary infringement of performers' rights, but the Act does not use that term and the protection provided is significantly weaker than the equivalent secondary infringing acts in relation to copyright:

- There is no equivalent to s 23(d), distributing otherwise that in the course of a business where this has an economic impact.

- Further, there is a specific defence under s 184(2) of 'innocent acquisition': where the alleged infringer did not know, and had no reason to believe, that the recording was an illicit recording, they can only be liable for damages not exceeding a reasonable payment in respect of it (ie not an injunction).

✅ *Looking for extra marks?*

This is much more favourable to importers and re-sellers when compared to the equivalent copyright provisions: even if they can claim lack of knowledge, the rights **owner** can write to give them that knowledge. With copyright, this can leave an importer or re-seller substantially out of pocket as a result of unsold stock. In the case of performers' rights, the stock can be sold off to cover costs, though the 'reasonable payment' will no doubt eliminate any profit margin.

Rights that protect against exploitation of performers

The two rights in the following sections provide some protection for performers against having to sign their rights away completely at the time of the performance.

The right to equitable remuneration (s 182D)

The right to equitable remuneration is required by the Directive, but is not characterized as a property right. It provides performers with a right to receive remuneration *from the owner of sound recording copyright in a recording of their performance*, provided the sound recording has been 'commercially published'. Commercial publication is defined in s 175 and includes making available electronically (s 182D(1A)).

The right to equitable remuneration arises whenever a commercially published recording is played in public or broadcast. The amount of remuneration can be settled by the Copyright Tribunal if the performer and the recording company cannot agree. While the other rights a performer has can be assigned or licensed in return for a lump sum, the right to equitable remuneration cannot be assigned (other than to a collecting society for the purpose of collecting the remuneration). Thus, if a recording achieves commercial success, the performer(s) are guaranteed a share in that success.

The right to equitable remuneration in respect of the rental right (s 191G)

While the s 182D right only applies to sound recordings, the right to equitable remuneration in respect of the rental rights applies to all recordings of performances, so includes film actors as well as musicians.

Where a performer has assigned their rental right (a performer's property right, so assignable) in relation to a sound recording or a film, the performer will have a right to equitable remuneration in the rental right that is non-assignable and with provisions relating to the fixing of the remuneration broadly similar to those applying under s 182D. One important difference is that there is an express acknowledgement in the statute (s 191H(4)) that remuneration by way of a lump sum may amount to equitable remuneration under s 191G.

Rights of record companies—'recording rights'

In ss 185–190, the Act also gives rights (known as 'recording rights') to the holder of exclusive recording rights. Section 185(1) defines such a person as someone who, as a result of a contract,

> is entitled to the exclusion of all other persons (including the performer) to make recordings of one or more of his performances with a view to their commercial exploitation.

To have recording rights, they must also be a qualifying person.

The consent of the recording rights holder or of the performer is required for the recording of a performance that is subject to an exclusive recording contract (s 185—equivalent to the s 182 right for performers). Recording rights are also infringed by:

- showing, playing in public, or communicating a recording (s 187—equivalent to the s 183 right for performers);

- importing or dealing in illicit recordings (s 188—equivalent to the s 184 right for performers). Section 197 defines 'illicit recording' for this purpose as one made without the consent of either the recording rights holder or the performer. There are similar provisions in relation to innocently acquired recordings as for s 184.

The effect of these provisions is that a performer may give consent to a recording, showing, etc that others can rely on, even if their recording contract does not permit this. Of course, this may result in the recording company having a right of action in contract against the performer.

Defences to infringement of the rights

CDPA, Sch 2 contains a number of defences to performers' rights infringement. These follow closely the defences to infringement of copyright as they relate to copyright in sound recordings and films—see Chapter 2. In particular, there are defences for:

- temporary copies;
- research and private study (since 1 June 2014);
- criticism, review, quotation (since 1 October 2014), and reporting current events;
- caricature, parody, or pastiche (since 1 October 2014);
- incidental inclusion.

There is a defence to a damages claim (but no other remedy) in relation to the property rights where the infringer did not know, and had no reason to believe, that rights existed in the recording (s 191J(1)). (In relation to the non-property rights, a defendant would be unlikely to infringe in such a case, as they would lack the necessary mental element.)

Duration of the rights (s 191)

Performer's rights last for 50 years, or 50 years from the date on which copies of the performance are released if they are released in that time. However, if a copy of the performance by an EEA national is released by way of a sound recording during the 50 years, the duration is 70 years from the date of release.

Exploitation of performers' rights

The distinction between property rights and non-property rights

The main difference between property and non-property rights is that property rights can be assigned by the performer; non-property rights cannot, and will remain enforceable by the performer—ss 191A–191E.

Property rights all involve the commercial exploitation of recordings of performances: copying them, placing them on the market, broadcasting via a recording, and making a recording available electronically.

Non-property rights, by contrast, involve the performer's basic right to decide whether and on what terms to give permission for the initial recording or broadcast of the performance, and the acts of secondary infringement in relation to illicit recordings.

The effect of the separation of the rights means that a performer may give consent to a performance being recorded, but that will not imply consent to that recording being exploited commercially by reproduction, publication, broadcast, and so on. Anyone wishing to exploit a recording of a performance in this way will have to do a deal with the performer in relation to their property rights.

Exploitation of performers' rights in practice

In most situations the producer of a sound recording or film will need to enter into a contract with the performer(s) to hire their services. As the owner of the economic rights in the recording or film, they will also be in a position to exploit the performance by use of the recording or film. This is why the legal protection of performers is closely linked with sound recording and film copyright.

In the case of the music industry, the record company will typically ensure that all performers sign agreements in industry-approved terms which, in return for the performer's fee:

- give permission for the recording of the performance (and broadcast if this is needed);

- assign the performers' property rights (so the record company can make copies of the master recording and distribute it via physical copies and electronically);

- make arrangements for a payment in respect of the right to equitable remuneration to be made to the performer (see Chapter 2—the record company will receive royalties via Phonographic Performance Ltd (PPL) when the recording is performed or broadcast; a small slice of this will effectively be passed on to the performer).

In the case of the film industry, actors typically give permission and assign all their rights in the same way, but there are two ways the law makes life easier for film producers: by s 191F the rental right is presumed to be assigned where there is agreement as to recording of the performance, and, as we have already seen, the right to equitable remuneration that arises from this may be compensated for by a lump sum. Thus, minor part actors and film extras can be paid a single sum, and that will deal with everything.

In film or music recording cases, major talent may be able to negotiate different terms (possibly including a share of income), depending on the parties' bargaining positions.

Litigation, remedies, and offences

Exclusive licensees of the property rights can sue. In relation to all the rights, the normal remedies are available. In relation to performers' property rights, additional damages are available under s 191J(2).

Performers' moral rights

Performers' moral rights were introduced into **CDPA, ss 205C–205N** in 2006 in order to implement the **WIPO Performances and Phonograms Treaty** (to which the UK, the EU, and most EU states are signatories). The rights (which only apply to qualifying performances) are described in the following sections. They do not impose too great a burden on the entertainment industry; for example, the rights will not apply to film actors at all in normal situations. (If they have a speaking part they will have the same rights as musicians in relation to a soundtrack dealt with separately.)

Both rights are non-assignable but can be waived for individual occasions or generally, and the right to be acknowledged as performer must be asserted. There are defences and exceptions analogous to those that apply to authors' moral rights, which protect the interests of broadcasters, news media, and so on. The limiting effect of these provisions on the usefulness of the rights is discussed in Chapter 4 in relation to authors' moral rights.

The right to be acknowledged as the performer

The right to be acknowledged as the performer arises whenever a person 'produces or puts on' a performance in public, when a performance is broadcast live, when sound recordings of the performance are communicated to the public, or when copies are issued to the public. (Note: 'communicated to the public' means broadcast or made available for streaming or download (s 20).) Thus, the right protects musicians in relation to the exploitation of recordings, but only protects actors in relation to live performance and broadcast.

Detailed provisions as to how the acknowledgement can be made are set out in s 205C(2). Where performers are known by a group name, reference to the group will satisfy the requirements.

The right to object to derogatory treatment of a performance

Derogatory treatment arises when the performance is broadcast live or a sound recording of it is played in public or communicated to the public. So actors are only protected in relation to live performance and broadcast; musicians are protected in relation to the communication of recordings, but not in relation to the distribution of copies of recordings. The right arises in relation to (s 205F):

> any distortion, mutilation or other modification that is prejudicial to the reputation of the performer.

What matters is the reputation of the performer, not that of the composer or lyricist: laying offensive lyrics over music, substituting rude words in the lyrics, or including 'bum' notes might be examples of treatment that might be held to be derogatory. For live acting performances, the addition of inappropriate subtitles or soundtrack might be objectionable.

🗨 Key debates

Topic	The extension to the term of musical performers' rights protection to 70 years
Author	EU Commission
Standpoint	Argues that as performers live longer, so their rights should last longer, and highlights the plight of session musicians—based on ideas of rights and fairness rather than economics.
Source	EU Commission's 2008 proposal (COM(2008) 464 final)
Author	Natalie Helberger, Nicole Dufft, Stef Van Gompel, and P Bernt Hugenholz
Standpoint	Argue that there is no economic basis for extending the term of protection for either performers or sound recordings, and that IP rights should not be extended unless there is a reason.
Source	'Never Forever, Why Extending the Term of Protection for Sound Recordings is a Bad Idea' [2008] 5 EIPR 174–181
Author	Ian Hargreaves
Standpoint	Found no evidence that performers would change their behaviour or decisions based on the copyright and performers' rights terms, and noted that most recordings have an economic life of less than ten years, though acknowledges that there may also be non-economic arguments.
Source	*Digital Opportunity* (TSO, 2011)

Exam question

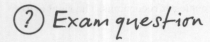

Problem question

Almost Flare are a Scottish tribute band to the 1970s glam-rock band the Flares. They play songs from the Flares' repertoire that are intended to sound, as far as possible, exactly like the original Flares recordings of the songs. Their management makes sure that all the necessary permissions in relation to the original Flares songs are obtained. Recently they went on a world tour that took in Russia. Chopper, Almost Flare's drummer, has been sent a DVD of a Russian documentary film about the Moscow club scene, including extensive footage of the band performing. He has discovered that the DVD is on sale at a specialist store in London, Sideways Records: he telephoned the shop, who told him that they got the DVDs from a dealer in Lisbon, Portugal. Chopper has discussed this with the band members. They all think that the DVD will help to publicize the band and are happy with the situation, but Chopper thinks his rights have been infringed and wants to do something more about it.

Have any of the band's rights been infringed, and can Chopper do anything about it himself? What remedies would be available and against whom?

See the Outline Answers section in the end matter for help with this question.

#6

Trade secrets and confidential information

Key facts

The law of trade secrets is purely judge-made law. The basic elements of the cause of action are:

- the claimant is in possession of information that is important and not in the public domain, or that is private;

- they impart that information to someone else in conditions that place that person under a duty of confidence in relation to it, or someone obtains that information in circumstances where they should realize that it is confidential;

- the recipient of the information misuses it or threatens to misuse it, misuse being to publish the information or make use of it.

The law has developed into separate strands with their own particular rules:

- the basic law relating to trade secrets;

- special provisions relating to the conduct of employees and ex-employees;

- a separate branch of the law dealing with private and personal information.

Overview and history

The action for breach of confidence has its roots in the law of equity. The action has developed over the years into something resembling a common law cause of action, with a full range of remedies, but its equitable basis is still evident in the flexibility and discretion the judges exercise in deciding cases.

The **Human Rights Act** in 1998 required the courts to implement (among other things) the right to private and family life. The courts were able to do this, where the infringement alleged consisted of misuse of information, by extending the law of breach of confidence. Judges now treat this as a separate branch of the law of breach of confidence, with its own developing case-law. Special considerations also apply in relation to the employer–employee duty.

Revision tip

Always check when reading cases or commentary whether it is about the general duty of confidence, the employer–employee relationship, or the right to privacy. Many important concepts do not transfer between these areas.

Private or confidential information is protected in a number of different situations by statute (an example being the **Data Protection Act 1998**). But there is no general statutory right.

The trade secrets branch of the law

The elements of the cause of action are set out in the case of *Coco v Clark* [1968]. For there to be an action for breach of confidence there must be:

- information of a confidential nature;
- (that was) communicated in circumstances importing an obligation of confidence; and
- an unauthorized use of the information by the person to whom it was communicated.

The law has moved on considerably since that case and these elements are best thought of as headings under which to organize subsequent case-law developments.

Information of a confidential nature

Megarry J said in *Coco* that the information must 'have the necessary quality of confidence'. Subsequent cases have added further requirements in relation to the information sought to be protected. The cases tend to involve information in the following categories:

- technical information (industrial processes, recipes, and so on that are not made public by carrying on the business);

- business information—about new business ventures, projects, or products (secret until the new product, etc has been launched);
- detailed information about the day-to-day operations of an existing business, for example detailed costings, recent unpublished sales figures, market research data, and so on;
- state secrets.

However, any information is protectable if the legal test is met.

The body of information must be defined

An injunction that did not specify what the defendant was not supposed to do would be unenforceable, and the rules of civil procedure require a claimant to set out in their statement of case the facts they rely on. Thus, a claimant must set out what their confidential information is, and claimants who are unable or unwilling to do so will fail. Although generally court documents will be public, rules of procedure allow for documents containing confidential information to be kept back, and place other parties to the litigation under a strict duty of confidence in relation to any documents disclosed. So claimants should have no concern in bringing a claim.

APA Thomas v Mould [1968] 2 QB 913

FACTS: The claimants would not divulge details of their tax avoidance scheme (which they said had been taken in breach of confidence).

HELD: No remedy could be granted unless they did.

Ocular Sciences Ltd and another v Aspect Vision Care Ltd and others [1997] RPC 289

FACTS: The claimants struggled to identify what aspects of a large amount of technical information (which included much public domain material) was confidential.

HELD: This did not amount to a sufficient description of the information sought to be protected.

The information must be secret/not in the public domain

The concept of the 'public domain' in the law of trade secrets is a relative one.

Franchi v Franchi [1967] RPC 149

FACTS: The information was contained in a patent published in Belgium.

HELD: It was in the public domain because the people interested in the information (patent agents) knew to search in overseas patents.

The trade secrets branch of the law

✳✳✳✳✳✳✳✳✳✳

The information in *Franchi* was not public simply because it was published. Unlike in patent law, there is no strict rule that any publication, however obscure, places material in the public domain. In the important 'Spycatcher' series of cases (eg *Attorney-General v Observer and others [1990]*), information contained in an unpublished book was held not to be in the public domain. Only after the book had been published in the United States and a significant number of copies had been purchased in the UK was the information no longer secret—and then the injunctions initially granted were discharged.

Revision tip

Make sure you separate the concept of secrecy and the public domain as it applies to trade secrets law from the concept of 'made available to the public' as it applies in patents and designs law. They are different—see Chapters 7 and 8.

A problem arises where public domain information is organized or added to and the result is claimed to be a secret. This arose in the *Ocular Sciences* case discussed earlier. In *Coco*, Megarry J said that in such cases the claimant must have exercised some 'skill and ingenuity' to produce new information out of the old. Subsequent cases have developed this concept—see the following sections.

The information must be of the right type

Since *Coco*, a number of cases have held that not all information is protectable, even if it is secret: information that is vague, trivial, or unoriginal is unprotectable.

In the context of information concerning ideas for new business projects, the rule has emerged that the idea must be sufficiently worked-up and detailed to be implemented. Thus, in *Fraser v Thames TV [1983]*, a proposal for a fiction series that included character outlines and plot trajectories was protectable, whereas in *De Maudsley v Palumbo [1996]*, ideas for a night club (the defendant went on to found the Ministry of Sound in London) were not protectable as they were too vague and general.

The House of Lords in *Douglas and others v Hello! Ltd and others (No 3) [2007]* chose a different indicator for whether information was protectable: commercial value. In *Douglas*, the information sought to be protected was the events at a private celebrity wedding. It was held that unofficial photographs of the wedding contained confidential information even after official photographs and reports of it had been published (so much information about it was in the public domain). The basis for this was that:

- each separate photograph will contain slightly different information from other photographs of the same event (so unpublished ones contain fresh information);

- that information was protectable as it had commercial value—evidenced by the fact that the defendant magazine was willing to pay for it and devote full-page spreads to it in successive editions.

Revision tip

Do not mix up the House of Lords' decision in *Douglas* with the decisions in the lower courts. The lower courts also considered the privacy branch of the law, but the issues that reached the House of Lords concerned just the commercial exploitation of information and related to the trade secrets branch of the law.

The extent to which *Douglas* has changed or developed the law in this area is not clear. Though the information in that case appears trivial, the earlier cases can be argued to be consistent with it.

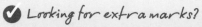 *Looking for extra marks?*

When discussing issues in this area, you should mention *Douglas* and consider both the earlier 'no trivia' rule and the *Douglas* 'commercial value' rule and, if appropriate, discuss the possible differences and further development of the *Douglas* doctrine.

A person under a duty of confidence

This is an area that has developed greatly through case-law since *Coco*. Each case will depend on its particular facts, but an *overarching principle* has emerged:

> A person is under a duty of confidence to another in respect of particular information if an honest person would regard themselves as bound by a duty if placed in that situation.

The test is partly objective and partly subjective. The standard of honesty is objective, but is applied to the particular circumstances and state of knowledge of the recipient of the information. The recipient is not under any duty to enquire about the information (*Thomas v Pearce*, discussed in 'Indirect relationships—'third parties').

Cases in this area can be categorized by the nature of the relationship between the claimant and the prospective defendant. However, note that the key question is whether a particular person owes a duty of confidence to another *in respect of particular information*. The nature of the relationship is an important factor in deciding whether a duty is owed, but it is only one factor. Other factors that may be relevant are:

- the nature of the information in which confidence is asserted (a recipient of trivial information is less likely to think any duty of confidence will arise);
- the precise circumstances in which the information is communicated or obtained (contrast a chance social encounter with a pre-arranged business meeting);
- any communications made at the time (eg a statement that the information was confidential).

Common types of relationship are dealt with in the following sections.

The trade secrets branch of the law

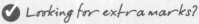

> ✅ **Looking for extra marks?**
>
> When considering a particular set of facts, make use of all the facts in deciding whether a duty exists, rather than just placing the relationship into a particular category where duties may arise.

Official bodies

Where legislation requires information to be given to or obtained by an official body (the police, regulatory authorities), they will be held to owe a duty of confidence in relation to any of that information that is confidential, though the information may be shared by the official body with others, where necessary given the purpose of the statute.

Hoechst v Chemiculture [1993] FSR 270

HELD: The Health and Safety Executive were under a duty of confidence in respect of information gathered under their statutory powers, but were not in breach of this by disclosing it to a third party with a mutual interest in achieving the purposes of the statute.

In many cases, the legislation giving the statutory powers will set out the scope of duties of confidence, but this is not necessary for one to arise.

Fiduciaries

A duty of confidence is part of the fiduciary duty. Fiduciary duties are owed by company directors to their company, by trustees to their beneficiaries, and by certain senior employees (see 'The special treatment of the employer–employee relationship'). Fiduciaries also owe further duties (including a positive duty to disclose relevant information).

Contractual terms as to confidentiality

Contracts often contain clauses imposing duties of confidence. These can be enforced in the usual way, although this cannot operate to protect otherwise unprotectable information—see 'Remedies and litigation'. A contractual term will also be a strong indicator that a duty is owed under the law of confidence. Conversely, a contractual term permitting use of information will mean that the cause of action cannot be made out.

Implied terms must also be considered. The rules implying terms into contracts, particularly the 'officious bystander' rule, will often imply a duty of confidence because many business relationships would be unworkable if there was no confidentiality. Professional advisor–client relationships are a good example: to give good advice the advisor needs information about the client, but the client will not give it unless confidentiality is assured. (Most professions—for example, doctors and lawyers—have professional rules about this, but a duty would arise in any event.) The employment relationship is a contractual one where a duty of confidence is implied: the duty of the employee is dealt with later in 'The special treatment of the employer–employee relationship', but employers also owe a duty in relation to information about the employee (often this will engage the right to personal privacy).

Cases involving information disclosed during the course of operation of a contract are generally argued under the law of confidence, rather than under the law of contract.

Ackroyds London v Islington Plastics [1962] RPC 97

FACTS: Designs for a new (not yet launched) product were given to a manufacturer as part of a contract to prepare production tooling.

HELD: The manufacturer was under a duty of confidence in respect of them.

Non-contractual business relationships

Business negotiations may require the exchange of information, and this increases the likelihood of a duty of confidence arising. In *Fraser* (see 'The information must be of the right type'), Mr Fraser 'pitched' ideas for the show to television executives, and a duty of confidence was held to exist.

Seager v Copydex (No 1) [1969] 1 WLR 809

FACTS: An inventor disclosed details of his invention during negotiations that concerned a different product.

HELD: A duty of confidence arose.

Social relationships

In *De Maudsley*, the information was disclosed during a dinner party. The court found that a duty of confidence did not arise in all the circumstances, but did not find that a duty could not arise at a dinner party, simply that such a duty did not arise at that particular party. In reality, there is a range of situations from the purely social, through 'networking' events to formal business meetings, and the full context must always be explored.

Duties of confidence can arise from purely social relationships, though normally the relationship must be a close one.

Stephens v Avery [1988] Ch 449

FACTS: Newsworthy personal information was disclosed in a close personal friendship (and Mrs Stephens stressed that it was confidential). The information was subsequently sold to the press.

HELD: A duty of confidence had arisen and had been breached as the relationship was of the type where confidences would be exchanged.

The trade secrets branch of the law

✱✱✱✱✱✱✱✱✱✱

(*Stephens* arose before the privacy branch of the law developed and the court applied traditional principles.)

Indirect relationships—'third parties'

Often the first recipient of information will pass it on to others, and they in turn may pass it on. The key to correctly analysing these situations is to remember the overarching principle and *look at the situation from the perspective of each recipient of the information to decide if they are under a duty*. It is not necessary to establish a chain of duties of confidence leading back to the claimant, or to identify how the information got where it ended up.

In *Thomas v Pearce* [2000], an employer accepting trade secrets from a new employee was held not to be bound by a duty on the basis that they may have been negligent in not realizing the truth, but not dishonest in the sense of 'turning a blind eye' to the source of the information. In *Attorney-General v Observer and others*, the newspaper editors were under a duty simply because the content of the document they received made it clear that it might contain state secrets.

No relationship at all—eavesdroppers and spies

The law also protects against a stranger obtaining information, rather than someone being given it—that is, against spying.

Breach of the duty

The duty is breached by the *misuse* of confidential information. This distinction is important legally, as **TRIPs Agreement, Art 39** requires states to protect undisclosed information, including against being acquired.

Misuse means:

- making the information public (this was the issue in cases such as *Douglas* and *Spycatcher*);
- using the information for one's own purposes (this was the issue in *Seager v Copydex*).

The claimant must show that the use or publication of information by the defendant can be traced back to the information that was disclosed in breach of a duty of confidence.

CMI-Centers for Medical Innovation GmbH and another v Phytopharm Plc [1999] FSR 235

FACTS: The claimant could only show that the defendant was working in the same field as that covered in the allegedly disclosed information, though there was information relevant to that field in the public domain, which the defendant could have relied on.

HELD: The claimant had failed to establish a breach.

The special treatment of the employer–employee relationship

In law, an employment relationship is a particular type of contractual relationship between two parties. The special rules set out here will not generally apply to a contract for services that is not an employment contract.

The general principles outlined earlier apply to the duty employees and ex-employees owe to their (former) employer, with two important modifying factors:

- other duties arising from the employment relationship are also relevant during employment;

- public policy considerations affect the duty owed once the relationship ends.

See Figure 6.1.

Note that express terms in a contract of employment can change the situation within legal constraints, which are explained in the following sections.

Duties of employees while employed

The basic duty all employees owe to their employer is a duty of 'faithful service': to do their best while at work and not to do anything that would damage the employer's interests. In *Faccenda Chicken v Fowler* [1987] it was said that, in relation to confidential information:

> The duty of fidelity includes the duty not to disclose the employer's affairs to his detriment and the duty not to misuse his employer's property, for example lists and plans. The duty not to disclose may be the same as saying that the protected information is confidential.

Figure 6.1 The different duties of the employee

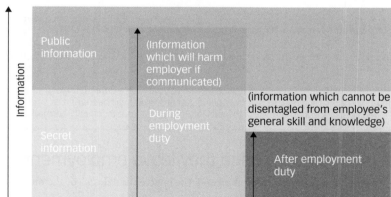

The special treatment of the employer–employee relationship
****

While employees are free to run their own businesses in their spare time, if those businesses compete with their employer that will be a breach of the duty. Preparations to set up a competing business will not necessarily amount to a breach:

Universal Thermosensors v Hibben [1992] 1 WLR 840

HELD: The following amounted to breaches of an employee's duty: contacting potential customers, poaching company employees, and taking information (on documents, or by downloading) for outside purposes (eg setting up a new business).

The effect of this duty is that many activities which involve company information and which would not amount to a breach of confidence under the law set out earlier may nevertheless be a breach of the employee's duty.

The employee's duties may be limited by the contract of employment. The contract (and surrounding documents, such as handbooks and so on) may also influence what information is caught by the duty of confidence by informing the employee of what categories of information the employer regards as secret (an application of the general principles noted earlier).

The public interest defence (and considerations of the employee's human rights) may limit the scope of the employee's duties, dealt with in a later section. 'Whistle-blowers' are protected against certain disciplinary actions by their employer by ss 43A–43L of the Employment Rights Act 1996.

Employees owing a fiduciary duty

Fiduciary duties, in addition to imposing a duty of confidence, impose on the employee a duty of disclosure of any information that might benefit the employer. This makes even *preparing* to compete difficult as any good business leads must be disclosed—they effectively 'belong' to the employer. The fiduciary duty is exclusive to the employer.

Company directors owe a fiduciary duty to their company (which may also be their employer).

Helmet Integrated Systems v Tunnard [2006] EWCA Civ 1735, [2007] IRLR 126

FACTS: A salesperson whose duties involved gathering data about competitors kept technical product information for his future business.

HELD: Employees whose duties include hallmarks of a fiduciary (eg a duty to disclose information and vulnerability of the employer to that duty being complied with) will be treated as fiduciaries. Mr Tunnard owed fiduciary duties in relation to sales information but not technical information.

Duties of employees once they leave employment

Once the employment relationship is at an end, the contractual duties of the employer cease, but:

The special treatment of the employer–employee relationship

- any contractual terms expressed to last after the employment ceases may be enforceable—see 'The use of restrictive clauses and "garden leave" clauses';
- the basic law of confidence still applies, so the employee will still owe a duty to keep secrets secret; but
- that duty is restricted by public policy considerations.

The public policy considerations stem from both a consideration of the rights of workers to use their skills to earn a living, and from the desirable objective of a free employment market. The result is explained in *Faccenda*:

- The duty of confidence cannot be enforced to prevent the ex-employee from using their skill and knowledge in their trade, even though they may have learned this as a result of their employment.

- Important confidential information other than that noted above remains protectable by applying the law of confidence to the situation, but trivial information is not protectable.

In *Faccenda*, the protectable information was described as 'trade secrets'. 'Trade secrets' is also used as the name of the branch of the law of confidence dealing with commercial information.

Revision tip

Check the context in which you read the phrase 'trade secret'. Do not apply principles of protectable information to other contexts that apply only in the ex-employee context.

General principles apply to what information, acquired during employment, may be covered by the post-employment duty. In *Faccenda*, the following factors were considered important:

- the nature of the employment;
- the nature of the information itself;
- whether the employer impressed on the employee the confidentiality of the information; and
- whether the relevant information could easily be isolated from other information that the employee is free to use or disclose.

As it is based on public policy, the general principle that workers should be able to make use of their skill and labour in the workforce may also be applied in cases of non-employed contractors, where the role of the contractor is essentially that of an employee (eg individual contractors in the IT and creative industries).

The use of restrictive covenants and 'garden leave' clauses

Frequently, when an employer is aggrieved by the activity of an ex-employee, what they are really concerned about is competitive activity. The employer's commercial objectives *may* be achievable by enforcing restrictive covenants, if these were included in the contract of employment (they will never be implied). Typical restrictive covenants may try to prevent the employee:

- from being involved in a competing area of business, for a certain period, and within a certain geographical area (non-competition covenants);
- from doing business (either personally or as an employee) with people who were customers of the employer during the employee's employment (non-dealing covenants);
- from actively soliciting business from people who were customers of the employer (non-solicitation covenants);
- from enticing away employees of the employer (non-poaching covenants).

Herbert Morris Ltd v Saxelby [1916] 1 AC 688

HELD: Restrictive covenants are restraints of trade and therefore only enforceable (as a matter of contract law) if they are justified as no more restrictive than is necessary in order to protect a legitimate business interest of the employer.

The courts have held that legitimate business interests are:

- **goodwill** with customers;
- trade secrets (in the sense used in this section);
- relations with employees.

Where covenants are sought to be justified on the basis of protecting trade secrets, the employer must have trade secrets that would be protectable applying the *Faccenda* principles—so covenants cannot be used to protect information that would not otherwise be protectable.

Thus, the covenants need to be carefully drafted to be enforceable. Further consideration of the law in this area is beyond the scope of this book, but typically, for an ordinary employee, a six-month non-solicitation covenant is considered appropriate, with further restrictions appropriate for more senior or key employees.

Finally, if an employee has to give notice of leaving, they can be required to work out their notice period by not coming in to work and not contacting any fellow employee, customer, contact, etc. This is known as 'garden leave' (the employee does not have to dig the garden, just sit in it). The idea is to take the employee out of circulation so that, by the time they do leave, the information they have will be out of date and their replacement will have established relations with their business contacts. Thus, the damage they can do in their new job or business is limited. The right to impose garden leave can be included in the contract of employment, though it is not necessary.

The general principles of restraint of trade clauses apply to contracts with non-employees as well as with employees.

The privacy branch of the law

The **Human Rights Act 1988** imposes an obligation on public bodies (including the courts) to carry out their activities in a way that respects the rights given by the **European Convention on Human Rights**. The courts are affected by this when they interpret statutes and when they apply judge-made law, such as the law of confidence.

The aspects of the Convention rights that are relevant to the law of trade secrets are:

* the right to a private and family life in **Art** 8, which can be infringed by obtaining, publishing, and using information;

* the right to freedom of expression in **Art** 10, the exercise of which could involve publishing confidential information.

Campbell v MGN [2004] is now regarded as the key case in this area. Here the House of Lords confirmed that the law of confidence is extended (so that the courts comply with their duty under the Act) in the following ways:

* Information of a private nature is protectable if a reasonable person of ordinary sensibilities, placed in the same situation as the subject of the disclosure, rather than its recipient, would find the disclosure offensive.

* Publication of the information may be restrained even if the information would be regarded as in the public domain applying the law of confidence as it relates to trade secrets.

* People who come across such information (eg newspaper editors) are under a duty of confidence in respect of it.

Thus, the activities of newsworthy people (possibly of a trivial nature), carried on in public (thus arguably in the public domain) but on a private occasion (eg a family visit to the beach) may be restrained from publication, though a claim under the traditional law of confidence would not give protection in such a case.

Wainwright v Home Office [2003] UKHL 53, [2004] 2 AC 406

HELD: The **Human Rights Act 1998** did not create a cause of action for breaches of the right to a private and family life. The law of confidential information will only protect breaches that relate to the misuse of information (so did not apply where a person was strip-searched).

But note that the courts may find that a defence applies, which is discussed under the next heading.

Defences

The courts have always refrained from granting a remedy where to do so would not be in the public interest. Prior to the **Human Rights Act** the 'public interest defence' covered the disclosure of information where that disclosure was in the public interest. This included 'whistle-blowing' activities, such as exposing wrongdoing. In *Lion Laboratories v Evans* [1985] (see Chapter 2), the defence also applied to an action for breach of confidence brought by Lion alongside their copyright action. As with copyright, the courts will consider whether the nature and scope of the disclosure is justified by the public interest.

The **Human Rights Act** has required the courts to modify their approach to be compliant with human rights principles. The rights to a private and family life and to freedom of expression are qualified rights, which means that when they are enforced they must be balanced against other Convention rights (particularly each other) and against other legal rights, such as protectable trade secrets and legal duties of confidence.

In *HRH Prince of Wales v Associated Newspapers Ltd* [2006], the public interest in the subject matter of communications and the press's right to express their views had to be balanced against the right to confidentiality and privacy and the public interest in express duties of confidence (of the Prince's staff) being complied with.

A specific issue important to the press arose in *Campbell*. The claimant (model Naomi Campbell) was not able to enforce her right to privacy because the public face she presented to the world was at odds with her private life, so there was a public interest in the publication of material correcting that impression. But the extent of the material disclosed by the press went beyond what was necessary to achieve the public interest, so to that extent they were in breach of a duty of confidence.

Remedies and litigation

Interim and 'quia timet' injunctions

In many confidential information cases the claimant is concerned to keep secret information secret, and thus will apply for an interim injunction (see Chapter 1). Often a search order is applied to gather evidence. The basic rules governing the grant of interim injunctions are modified in some confidential information cases.

Section 12 of the Human Rights Act 1998 states that when a defendant's freedom of expression might be affected by the grant of an injunction, 'No . . . relief is to be granted . . . before trial unless the court is satisfied that the applicant is likely to establish that publication should not be allowed.' This amounts to a major change to the 'serious issue to be tried' part of the *American Cyanamid* test.

In cases to enforce a short restrictive covenant, or where the duration of the secrecy of the information is short, the grant of an interim injunction will decide the issue finally, since by the time of the trial the claimant will no longer be entitled to an injunction. In these cases, the court will do its best to decide the substantive issues as if it were the trial court.

In many cases, the misuse of the information will not yet have occurred, so technically there will have been no breach. 'Quia timet' injunctions (see Chapter 1) are very common in confidentiality cases.

The 'springboard doctrine'

One situation where the duration of the secrecy of information is short is where the information is soon to be published (eg a company's annual report). The court will not generally grant an injunction that lasts beyond the duration of the secrecy of the information, as to do so would be to restrain the defendant from doing something lawful, which others could do.

The 'springboard doctrine' is an exception to this. In some situations information is in the public domain in the sense of being available, but there will be a lead-time before lawful obtainers of the information can take advantage of it. For example, when a new product has been launched, imitation products may be made (subject to other IP rights) by a process of 'reverse engineering', but that takes time. A defendant who obtained design information in breach of confidence will be able to get a competing product to market quicker than lawful competitors. The courts have recognized this by granting injunctions extending beyond the time when the information is notionally public in order to deny defendants this advantage.

Vestergaard Frandsen and others v Bestnet Europe Ltd, and others [2011] EWCA Civ 424

HELD: The Court of Appeal approved the first instance judge's application of proportionality principles in deciding not to grant a springboard injunction. The **Enforcement Directive (2004/48/EC)** (see Chapter 1) required this as trade secrets were a form of intellectual property for the purposes of the Directive.

Dealings in trade secrets; information as property

The courts have confirmed on many occasions that secret information is not property, so spying is not theft unless physical items are taken (though other non-property offences may be committed). Contracts are commonly entered into relating to secret information by an exchange of promises:

- A promises to disclose secret information to B; and
- A and B exchange promises to keep that information secret (sufficient consideration);
- B may also pay money to A.

In this situation, B has been 'brought inside the circle of confidence' and (subject to any agreement with A about litigation) may be able to make out all the elements of the cause of action and so sue for breach of confidence itself. Thus, information can be transferred or licensed. This type of arrangement is very common in research and the development of technology and is crucial if technological developments are to be shared without prejudicing the chances of obtaining patent protection—see Chapter 7.

Whether a recipient of information is under a duty in respect of it depends on what the recipient knew and how an honest person would regard the situation (see 'A person under a duty of confidence'). Entrepreneurs and inventors should ensure that potential financiers or partners have signed a confidentiality undertaking before secret information is disclosed to them. This will increase the chances of the recipient being under a duty.

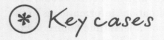

(✱) Key cases

Case	Facts	Principle
Coco v A N Clarke (Engineers) Ltd [1969] RPC 41	Coco had designed a motor-scooter engine, and negotiated with Clarke to license the design to them. The negotiations failed and Clarke went on to build a scooter engine. Coco alleged that this was a breach of a duty of confidence to him. The court found that Clarke owed a duty to Coco but that the Clarke design was based on publicly known features, so they were not in breach.	The key elements of the cause of action were established: – information of a confidential nature; – communicated in circumstances importing an obligation of confidence; – an unauthorized use of the information.
Attorney-General v Observer and others [1990] 1 AC 109 (HL)	A former MI6 spy, W, emigrated to Australia and published his memoirs there and in the United States. W was in breach of his duty to the UK government in doing this. Copies of the memoirs came into the possession of UK newspaper editors. The facts in the book included some clear state secrets. In time, many copies of the book were purchased by UK readers via mail-order from the United States.	The editors were under a duty of confidence to the government in relation to the state secret information because it was clear to a person reading the memoirs that the information was confidential. The information in the book entered the public domain once it had been widely purchased in the UK, and from then it was no longer a breach of duty for the newspapers to publish extracts.

Case	Facts	Principle
Fraser v Thames TV [1984] QB 44	F pitched an idea for a TV series (later broadcast as *Rock Follies*) about an all-female rock band. The proposal included character sketches, outlines of developing relationships, and other plot items.	The court found that the idea was sufficiently detailed to be worked up into a series and so was protectable information. (The other elements were there, so the claimant succeeded.)
Douglas v Hello! and others (No 3) [2007] UKHL 21, [2008] 1 AC 1	Mr and Mrs D sold exclusive rights to take photographs at their wedding and reception to *OK!* magazine, and required all guests to refrain from photography. *OK!* published its official photographs over a number of issues. A freelance photographer was able to gain access and take photographs. These were published by Hello! magazine at the same time and after *OK!*'s initial item on the wedding. Hello! had been outbid by *OK!* for the rights to photograph the wedding.	*Hello!* magazine were bound by a duty of confidence in relation to the photographs they received from the freelancer, as they knew of the arrangements for photographing the wedding. Even after *OK!*'s initial report of the wedding, the photographs in *Hello!*'s possession contained confidential information that was not in the public domain, as each different photograph of a scene contained detail that was not in other photographs. That different photographic information was protectable because it had value—*Hello!* had paid the photographer for the photos and considered it worth devoting space to them in its magazine.
De Maudsley v Palumbo [1996] EMLR 460	The parties attended a small dinner party at which De M mentioned to P ideas for a new style of night-club: open late legally, contemporary music, modern industrial style, a quality sound system, and separate areas, including a VIP area. P went on to found the Ministry of Sound club, which incorporated some of those features.	In all the circumstances, the dinner party conversation did not give rise to a duty of confidence on P's part: the test was objective, though the parties' understanding of their duty was a relevant factor. The information imparted was not sufficiently worked up to amount to protectable information as it was too vague. Business idea information must contain an element of originality and commercial attractiveness and be sufficiently well developed to be capable of actual realization.
Thomas v Pearce [2000] FSR 718	Mrs Pearce, an estate agent, moved from Mrs T's agency to a rival agency, D, and took with her lists of customers and potential clients. Mrs Pearce disclosed the list to an employee of D, Mrs Price, and D made use of it. The court found that Mrs Price had been careless in not checking where the information came from, but not dishonest.	A third party in Mrs Price's position did not owe a duty of care to investigate whether information they were given was someone else's confidential information. Provided they did not act dishonestly or turn a deliberate blind eye to the source of the information, they were not in breach.

Key cases

✳✳✳✳✳✳✳✳✳✳

Case	Facts	Principle
Faccenda Chicken v Fowler [1987] Ch 117	Fowler had been employed by Faccenda and had built up a van sales operation. He then left and set up his own chicken sales operation from a van. Faccenda alleged that Fowler used their confidential information in this new business, being information about the best routes to take between customers and information about the customers and their preferences as to the quality of chicken they purchased.	To be protected when an employee leaves employment, information needed to be secret, not part of the employee's general skill and knowledge, and not trivial. All the information Fowler used was contained in his head. It formed part of his general skill and knowledge about the chicken trade. Accordingly, it was not information that could be protected.
Campbell v MGN [2004] UKHL 22, [2004] 2 AC 457	Model Naomi Campbell took part in public campaigns against recreational drug use and supporting those affected by it. In the course of this she proclaimed a personal anti-drug stance. She was photographed in a public place entering premises at a time when an Addicts Anonymous meeting was taking place there, in order to address her personal drug addiction problem. A newspaper published the photograph and explained its significance in the copy.	The threshold test as to whether information was private was to ask whether a reasonable person of ordinary sensibilities, if placed in the same situation as the subject of the disclosure, rather than its recipient, would find the disclosure offensive. The threshold was met by the information about Ms Campbell's visit. This was the case despite the fact that the visit took place in public, and was required as a result of the **Human Rights Act** and Ms Campbell's right to a private and family life. There was a public interest in the publication of facts about Ms Campbell's addiction, to correct the impression given by her. The publication of the photographs went beyond what was in the public interest and was beyond the scope of the defence of public interest.
HRH Prince of Wales v Associated Newspapers Ltd [2006] EWCA Civ 1776, [2008] Ch 57	An aide to the Prince gave a newspaper a copy of a journal kept by the Prince of his private thoughts and impressions of an overseas visit to Hong Kong. The newspaper sought to publish extracts, which included disparaging remarks about the occasion and its participants, and claimed exercise of its freedom of expression.	The journal clearly contained private and confidential information and so the paper was under a duty of confidence. The public interest in the dissemination of information and the paper's right of freedom of expression had to be balanced against the Prince's right to privacy and the public interest in confidences being kept in a proportionate way in accordance with the doctrines of the ECHR. That balance lay in favour of the Prince in this case.

Key debate

Topic	The extension of the law of confidence since *Coco* and the impact of the *Douglas v Hello!* decision
Author	Hazel Carty
Standpoint	Argues that although recent cases in the area refer to *Coco* as the leading case, in fact the courts have developed an 'extra-*Coco* analysis' under the *Coco* headings, which Carty calls a 'merit-based' approach. The conduct of the claimant is judged to see if they took adequate steps to protect their information; the information is judged to see if it is worthy of protection; and the conduct of the defendant is judged; only defendants who have misbehaved are in breach.
	On this basis, argues that *Douglas* (HL) missed an opportunity to recognize this and re-formulate the law to make this merit-based approach more explicit (and to stop considering Coco as the leading authority), and that it was wrongly decided in not giving sufficient weight to the intrinsic merit of the information (which was trivial).
Source	'An Analysis of the Modern Action for Breach of Commercial Confidence: When is Protection Merited?' [2008] IPQ 416–455

Exam questions

Problem question

Henry is a salesman for Educational Supplies, a company that manufactures classroom equipment for use in primary schools. Henry got a birthday present recently, which was a rack for storing cookery utensils. Henry realized that this rack operated in a similar way to Educational's system for displaying students' work on classroom walls, only it was stronger. Henry had the idea that the cookery system would be useful in classrooms for displaying heavier items that students produced, such as pottery, and there would be a market for the product in the educational sector. He therefore approached the manufacturers, Stylish Cookwares, and suggested that they start an educational division, which he would manage. Stylish agreed to this and Henry immediately left his job at Educational and started a round of visits to his school contacts selling the Stylish product and other products that Stylish would purchase from other suppliers.

What can Educational do about Henry's and Stylish's activities?

See the Outline Answers section in the end matter for help with this question.

Exam questions
✱✱✱✱✱✱✱✱✱

Essay question

Critically evaluate the effect of the decision of the House of Lords in *Douglas and others v Hello! Ltd and others (No 3)* [2007] *UKHL 21* on the law of breach of confidence.

Online Resource Centre

To see an outline answer to this question visit www.oup.com/lawrevision/

#7
Patents

Key facts

Patents are granted for new technological developments ('inventions'). They are not granted for developments in the creative or non-technological arts (so a new and inventive play or novel is not patentable). Areas on the borderline between art and technology, such as computer programming and business methods, are the subject of difficulty and controversy. For a patent to be granted in Europe for an invention, the invention must be:

- in an area of technology and not fall within an excluded category;

- new, in the sense of not having been previously made available to the public anywhere in the world;

- contain an inventive step—that is, it must not have been obvious to a skilled person working in the same field of technology;

- explained in the published patent so that it can be put into practice by others;

- described in a **claim(s)** in the published patent, which set the technological scope of the monopoly;

- not be contrary to public order or morality.

Patents last for 20 years from application, but may be revoked at any time on the ground that the invention does not meet the requirements for patentability. Manufacturing or dealing in products, or carrying out processes, as described in the patent's claims infringes the patent.

Overview and history

Patents originated as the grant of 'letters patent' by the Crown, which gave monopolies over areas of trade. These monopolies were not necessarily related to technological innovation. Parliament passed the Statute of Monopolies in 1624 to limit the power of the Crown to grant monopolies to inventions, and only for fixed terms. This was the birth in the UK of the modern concept of a patent as a monopoly granted by the state, for a limited period, and for a defined activity, as a reward for technological innovation. The current UK statute governing patents is the Patents Act 1977 (PA 1977), passed to implement the European Patent Convention (EPC).

Unlike copyright, where both economic and individual rights arguments are important, the main theoretical reasons for the grant of patents are economic: if inventors were not granted patents, they would attempt to keep their technology to themselves. In the case of inventions where secrecy was not possible (eg product designs), there would be little incentive to invest in research and development, as successful products could be copied. Unlike copyright, patents protect ideas—the combination of technological ideas contained in the claims.

The term and scope of the rights granted are the same for all patents, whether the invention is a cunning design for a door-latch that could be developed and built in a month, or a new drug that required millions of pounds worth of research, development, and testing to bring to market. Economic theory would suggest that the term of the monopoly should reflect the social value of or investment put into the technological development, and that a 'one-size-fits-all' patent is likely to under-reward some inventions, while giving an overly generous monopoly to others.

The provisions of the law that require inventors to disclose how to put their invention into effect in their patent application, and the requirement that applications must be published if they are to proceed, reflect this theory. Publishing the underlying technology enables further developments to be built on it by others—society receives a benefit in return for granting the monopoly.

The skilled person

Questions of fact relevant to patent law (such as **obviousness**, what a disclosure teaches) often require an understanding of the technology involved. The law makes use of the hypothetical 'skilled person' to answer these questions. The 'skilled person':

- is involved in the field of technology of the invention;
- may be a team of people if more than one field is involved;
- is aware of all material that is in the public domain in that field and 'common general knowledge' relating to the field; but
- has no inventive capacity—so will not, for example, combine ideas from two different published sources unless they cross-refer.

In practice, the courts rely on expert opinion evidence to establish what the skilled person would know and be capable of.

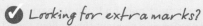

✅ Looking for extra marks?

As a lawyer, your opinion on technological matters will be unreliable. Try to frame your answers in terms of a question—making use of any detailed facts you have been given and involving the skilled person—that requires an answer—even if you do go on to offer an opinion about it yourself. This chapter explains the precise questions that are relevant to each legal area.

The European Patent Convention

Thirty-eight European states are currently signatories to the EPC, including all the EU states. The Convention:

- sets out a system of substantive patent law (law about the granting and infringement of patents);
- sets up the European Patent Office (EPO), which is located in Munich, Germany, and which grants patents in accordance with that law;
- requires states to give effect to the patents so granted as if they were national patents.

The key features of the system are as follows:

- States may still grant patents through their national patent offices. Inventors can choose whether to obtain protection in a particular state by making an application to the patent office for that state or via an application to the EPO.
- When the EPO grants a patent, it takes effect as a bundle of national patents in those states that the applicant designated when they applied. An inventor cannot apply for a national patent and a European patent designating that state for the same invention.
- After the EPO grants a patent there is a nine-month period during which anyone may oppose the grant of the patent by applying to the EPO. If this opposition is successful, all the national patents in the bundle originally granted are revoked.
- Aside from such opposition, the EPO loses all jurisdiction over a patent once it is granted. The patents in the bundle take effect in all respects as if they are national patents and so enforcement litigation, assignments and licences, and revocation proceedings take effect according to local procedures, though the provision of the Convention must apply, through national implementing laws, to issues of validity and infringement.

The system is an imperfect compromise that arises from the reluctance of the states, at the time of signing the Convention, to relinquish powers to the EPO. This system has weaknesses when viewed from an EU perspective as it does not fully reflect a free internal market in goods. A product may be held to infringe the local part of a European patent in one state, but the same product may be held not to infringe in another. One part of a European patent may be held invalid by a state, while a different state may find that its part of the patent is valid. The cost and expense of obtaining and enforcing a patent throughout the EU is greater than it would be for a single state. This has led to calls and action for reform—see generally *UnilinBeheer BV v Berry Floor NV* [2007].

Relationship between national laws, the Convention, and the EPO

The signatory states to the **EPC** form the European Patent Organisation, which oversees the operation of the Treaty and the EPO. This organization *is not part of the EU*, but the harmonizing effect of the EPC has meant that the EU has focused its efforts on harmonizing other areas of IP law. Nevertheless, the EU has sought to harmonize patent law in two areas: biotechnology (it succeeded in passing a Directive) and **computer programs**, where the attempt failed before the EU Parliament.

EU states including the UK have changed their laws for national patents (patents granted by their national patent offices) to reflect the provisions of the EPC—strictly it was not the EPC that required this, but another Convention that never actually took effect, the Community Patent Convention. In the UK, **PA 1977, s 130(7)** lists those sections that are to be interpreted in accordance with the Convention (all the main substantive provisions of patent law).

The EPO has an internal route of appeal from an examiner to the Technical Boards of Appeal (TBAs). An Extended Board of Appeal (EBA) may hear appeals on issues of interpretation of the Convention from a TBA. Although national courts are not bound by the case-law of the TBAs and EBA, in practice they try to follow it. They also take notice of decisions from the courts and patent offices of other Member States with the aim of legal harmony.

There is no single binding court of appeal on issues of interpretation of the Convention. The interpretation of the Convention can, and does in some areas, diverge between states. This is another criticism of the system.

Actavis UK Ltd v Merck & Co Inc [2008] EWCA Civ 444, [2008] RPC 26

HELD: Compliance with the jurisprudence of the TBAs and EBA is a valid ground on which the Court of Appeal may depart from its earlier judgments as long as the EPO jurisprudence provides a clear statement of the law and is not clearly wrong.

The future plans for patents in the EU

Two EU Regulations have been passed to implement a scheme by which the EU will, in effect, become an EPO state and so an EPO application will result in a single patent ('unitary patent') covering the EU states (as well as other single patents for other EPC states). These will not come into effect until the states have ratified the European Patent Litigation Agreement (EPLA), which sets up a single patent court for hearing disputes involving unitary patents.

Brexit poses a difficulty for this scheme, as the UK was to host one of the courts. The Minister has indicated that the UK intends to go ahead and ratify the EPLA, though the precise way forward for the scheme remains unclear. It is possible that this scheme will become operational during the currency of this edition. It will address many of the criticisms of the current regime, though it has been the subject of criticism itself.

Revision tip

The patent system in Europe is different from the systems for the two other registered rights—trade marks and designs—which are harmonized by EU law and where the European granting office is an EU institution. Make sure you can separate the two systems—see Chapters 8 and 9.

✔ *Looking for extra marks?*

There is detailed and updated information about the new system on the EPO website:
http://www.epo.org/law-practice/unitary.html
and the Court's website:
http://unified-patent-court.org/
You should check on the latest status of the new system.

International conventions

The **Paris Convention** deals with the priority period and equal treatment of nationals in applying for patents. The **Patent Cooperation Treaty** provides a mechanism for applying for patents with a single international application.

The only worldwide treaty that provides for international harmonization (beyond Europe) of substantive patent law is the **TRIPs Agreement**. This requires states to grant patents where the basic elements of patentability, as set out in 'Key facts', are met. It requires patents to be granted 'in all areas of technology' and does not permit any exclusions (except on morality grounds). See 'Patentable subject matter' for how the excluded areas set out in the **EPC** can be reconciled with this.

Patent structure, applications, and the international patent system

Structure of a patent

Throughout the world, patents (the public documents that formally describe the right) contain the same basic elements:

- a section containing details of the patent—when it was filed, any priority claims, the inventor, the applicant, and so on;
- a description of the invention, which teaches the skilled person how to put the invention into effect (how to make a product or implement a process);
- optional drawings or tables, which can contribute to the description; and
- one or more claims that set out the precise technological scope of the monopoly granted by the patent.

Unless an alleged infringer is making or doing something that falls within the scope of a claim, there is no infringement. Claims may describe things (useful articles, machines, and so on), known as 'product claims', or processes (sequences of steps to go through to achieve a particular result), known as 'process claims'. The drawings or description may be used to interpret the claims, but it is the claims that define the technological scope of the monopoly.

The procedure before the EPO is set out in Figure 7.1; procedure before the UK Patent Office is broadly similar.

Fees are payable at various stages in the process, and upon grant and subsequently to renew the patent. The inventor, if they apply for a search promptly, should be able to withdraw their application before the deadline for it to be published if the search report is unfavourable. There may be useful trade secrets in the application, so there is no point in allowing it to be published if a patent is unlikely to result.

Obtaining patents internationally

Most countries have signed the **Patent Cooperation Treaty**, which is administered by WIPO. This Treaty permits 'international applications' to be made to one of a number of national patent offices, which are authorized by WIPO to receive them:

- The applicant files their application, designating those countries in which patent protection is sought—this application can claim priority from an earlier application, and the EPO may be included as a designated area.
- A search is carried out and an international search report is prepared.
- Optionally an advisory examination is carried out.

Figure 7.1 EPO application procedure

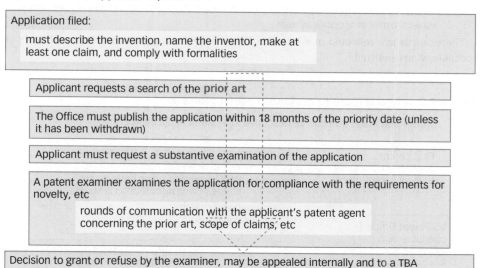

- The international search report is forwarded to the national patent offices of the designated countries, which rely on the international search when carrying out their own examination according to their own procedures and patent laws.

Where a high level of international coverage is required, this procedure saves cost as the national patent offices charge lower fees for the final stage of the procedure (as they do not have to carry out a search). See Figure 7.2.

Patentable subject matter

Article 52 of the EPC states:

(1) European patents shall be granted for any inventions, in all fields of technology, provided that they are new, involve an inventive step and are susceptible of industrial application.

(2) The following in particular shall not be regarded as inventions within the meaning of paragraph 1:

(a) discoveries, scientific theories and mathematical methods;

(b) aesthetic creations;

(c) schemes, rules and methods for performing mental acts, playing games or doing business, and programs for computers;

(d) presentations of information.

(3) Paragraph 2 shall exclude the patentability of the subject-matter or activities referred to therein only to the extent to which a European patent application or European patent relates to such subject-matter or activities as such.

These words are reflected in s 1(1)–(3) of the PA 1977, though the words 'in all fields of technology' are omitted.

Figure 7.2 A typical route to worldwide patent protection

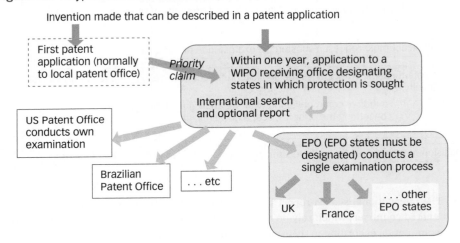

There must be 'an invention'

The courts and the EPO have (very rarely) interpreted the requirement for an invention as having an independent meaning; that is, even if something is not expressly excluded it may still be refused a patent on the ground that it is not an invention.

Recent approaches to topics such as excluded subject matter and sufficiency of claims make it unlikely that courts will need to resort to this in future.

'Capable of industrial application'

This requirement overlaps with the exclusion of discoveries (discussed next). Industrial application means that the claimed invention can be carried out in any industry; that is, you can make a product that you can sell or hire, or carry out a service in return for money. (Whether it would be profitable to do so is not relevant.)

Discoveries of properties of nature or new chemicals are not considered per se to be capable of industrial application, but if a practical application of the discovery is disclosed in the application, that is patentable.

Max-Planck/BDP1 Phosphatase (T870/04) [2006] EPOR 14

FACTS: A new chemical was discovered and the patent taught how to make it, but only vague suggestions were given as to how it might be used.

HELD: Industrial applicability had to be disclosed in or apparent from the specification, which was not the case here.

Medical inventions

EPC, Art 53(c) and PA 1977, s 4A exclude from patentability methods of treatment of humans or animals. This exclusion is expressly limited: substances or compositions used in such treatment are patentable—so, for example, drugs and medical equipment can be patented.

The excluded categories

The EPO has developed a general principle that patents should only be granted for technical things, and has stated that the excluded things in Art 52 are examples of non-technical things. Until it changed its approach in the case *PBS Partnership/Controlling Pension Benefits System* [2002] (*'Pensions'*), the EPO developed the doctrine of the 'contribution to the art' in interpreting Art 52: inventions were excluded if the contribution to the art did not lie in a technical area. This required looking beyond how the claim was drafted and finding out what the invention actually made available that was not available before.

Koch & Sterzel/X-ray Apparatus (T26/86) [1988] EPOR 72

FACTS: A new x-ray machine only differed from prior machines in the software that it ran, but it resulted in a better functioning x-ray machine.

HELD: The new machine made a technical contribution to the art, so it was not excluded.

The UK Court of Appeal followed the contribution approach in interpreting s 1 of the PA 1977 in *Merrill Lynch*:

Merrill Lynch Inc's Patent Application [1989] RPC 561

FACTS: The claim was framed as 'a data processing system which . . .'

HELD: The claim was refused because the technical contribution to the art of the system did not extend beyond computer programming.

Patentable subject matter

✱✱✱✱✱✱✱✱✱

The UK courts have never accepted that all the excluded things are of a non-technical nature (eg computer programs).

In *Pensions*, the EPO changed doctrine decisively to what has become known as the 'any hardware' approach. The TBA reinterpreted **Art 52** and held that, as long as the claim was drafted to cover an item of hardware or a process using it (eg a computer programmed in a particular way), then the invention was not excluded. However, the EPO went on to confirm that when assessing whether there was **novelty** and an inventive step, only technical inventiveness counted, so if the development was confined to the field of computer programming, there would be no inventive step. The effect is that the investigation into technical content takes place at a different stage of the examination process (when considering novelty and obviousness, not when considering patentable subject matter).

The UK courts did not follow the EPO in this area. The UK judiciary and patent office were resistant to the 'any hardware' approach and felt that the EPO cases were inconsistent (meaning that they should not change their approach—see 'Relationship between national laws, the Convention, and the EPO'). The courts have instead refined the contribution approach.

Aerotel v Telco Holdings Ltd [2006] EWCA Civ 1371, [2007] RPC 7

The correct approach requires:

- properly construing the claim;
- identifying the actual contribution;
- asking whether it falls solely within the excluded subject matter; and
- checking whether the actual or alleged contribution is in fact technical in nature.

The UK courts do not ignore developments in excluded areas when considering novelty and obviousness (*Merrill Lynch*, discussed above).

The EPO has now clarified its approach:

President's Reference/Computer Program Exclusion (G3/08) [2010] EPOR 36 (EBA)

HELD: The *Pensions* approach is the correct one and the EBA helpfully summarized the doctrine to be adopted when deciding patentable subject matter (described earlier).

Thus there is no longer any reason for the Court of Appeal not to follow *Pensions*, and *Actavis* suggests it should, but it has not done so:

HTC Europe Co Ltd v Apple Inc [2013] EWCA Civ 451

HELD: *Symbian* remained the correct approach (discussed under 'Computer programs and business methods') and the *Aerotel* four-step approach, though it was not actually necessary, was valid. The Court of Appeal considered *G3/08*, but declined to follow it.

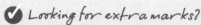

✔ Looking for extra marks?

You should apply the correct test (UK or EPO) in this area or consider both if the forum is unclear. But note that the actual outcome of any particular case will probably be the same. The difference between the approaches lies in when, and precisely how, during the patent examination process prior art is considered and technical content is looked for—inventions that lack technical content will be refused whatever test is used. The 'any hardware' approach does *not* mean 'anything is patentable'!

Specific technologies—patentability issues

Computer programs and business methods

Pensions concerned a computer-implemented business method, and the TBA found that any inventive step was confined to those (non-technical) areas. Many recent cases involve computerized ways of doing business, particularly where networks are involved.

Hitachi/Auction Method (T258/03) [2004] EPOR 55 (EPO)

FACTS: The claims were for a method of conducting an online auction (implemented in a computer program).

HELD: There was no technical inventive step in devising an auction method to work around the technical limitations of online bidding.

In *Symbian Ltd v Comptroller General of Patents* [2008], the Court of Appeal applied the 'contribution approach' and held that an invention in the field of computer technology contained a technical contribution when the invention resulted in a 'new type of computer'— even if the invention was essentially implemented solely in software.

Biotechnology

European states had different approaches to the patenting of biotechnological material. In 1998, the EU passed a Directive on biotechnological inventions (**Directive 98/44/EC**), with the aim of harmonizing the law in this area and promoting the EU biotechnology industry. This has been implemented by the EU states, and its provisions incorporated into the **EPC** and its implementing regulations. The key aspects of the Directive are its effect on what can be patented in this field. The implementing provisions are in **Sch A2 to the PA 1977**.

The Directive:

- applies to 'biological material', which it defines as 'any material containing genetic information and capable of reproducing itself or being reproduced in a biological system';

- confirms that inventions involving such material are patentable subject to some exclusions and general patent law principles;

Patentable subject matter

✳✳✳✳✳✳✳✳✳✳✳

- places a boundary between traditional plant-breeding and animal husbandry techniques ('biological processes' that are not patentable because they are not the products of such techniques) and 'microbiological processes', which involve biological material, and which are patentable, as are the products of microbiological processes;
- in support of the previous distinction, states that 'Inventions which concern plants or animals shall be patentable if the technical feasibility of the invention is not confined to a particular plant or animal variety' (Art 4(2));
- states how certain patent law principles should apply to biological material:
    - naturally occurring substances can be patented if isolated from their natural environment by a technical process (Art 3(2));
    - where a patent is sought for a gene or gene sequence, the industrial applicability of it must be disclosed (Art 5(3)—arguably simply discovering a gene would be unpatentable as a 'mere discovery' in any event);
    - where reproductive material is supplied with the permission of the patent owner, the patent is infringed by the use of material reproduced from that, subject to a defence for farmers breeding from seed and livestock for their own purposes (Arts 8–11).

The human body at various stages of its development and 'the simple discovery of' an element of the body including a gene sequence is not patentable. Where an element is isolated from the body, that may be patentable (Art 5).

The Directive contains further exclusions based on morality considerations in Art 6(2)— the following are unpatentable:

- processes for cloning human beings;
- processes for modifying the germ line genetic identity of human beings;
- uses of human embryos for industrial or commercial purposes;
- processes for modifying the genetic identity of animals, which are likely to cause them suffering without any substantial medical benefit to man or animal, and also animals resulting from such processes.

Brüstle v Greenpeace eV (C-34/10) [2012] 1 CMLR 41

FACTS: The claims covered use of human embryos for scientific research purposes.

HELD: This amounted to industrial or commercial use in the context of a patent (patents imply industrial and commercial exploitation). Only 'use for therapeutic or diagnostic purposes which are applied to the human embryo and are useful to it' would be patentable.

The last bullet point in the previous list was also a relevant consideration in the *Oncomouse* case, where the suffering of the mice (they were predisposed to cancer) was outweighed by the benefit to medical research into cancer cures and treatments.

The Directive in part reflects the finding in *Onco-mouse*:

Harvard/Onco-mouse [1991] EPOR 525 (EPO)

FACTS: A mouse was genetically modified to be prone to cancer, causing suffering to the mouse but being of benefit to medical research.

HELD: The mouse was patentable because the genetic modification could also be applied to other species of mammal. Although the mice suffered, there were medical benefits.

WARF/Stem cells (G2/06) [2009] EPOR 15 (EPO EBA)

HELD: The biotechnology-specific exclusions were examples of the application of the general morality exclusion (see the following section) and were consistent with it. A process that necessarily involved (at the time of filing the patent) the destruction of human embryos was unpatentable under the equivalent **EPC** provision to **Art 6(2)(c)**.

The general morality exclusion

Article 53(a) of the EPC and s 1(3) of the PA 1977 state that patents shall not be granted for inventions that 'are contrary to public order or morality'.

The specific morality-related exclusions for biotechnology were noted in 'Specific technologies—patentability issues'. Outside the biotechnological field, examples of inventions excluded on this ground are rare. Patents for lethal weapons are not excluded, for example.

Novelty

Basic principles

To be new, an invention must not form 'part of the state of the art' (**PA 1977, s 4** and **EPC, Art 54**). The art is defined as anything made available to the public before the priority date of the patent. The effect of case-law from both the **EPC** and the **UK** courts on this topic is summarized in Figure 7.3.

These concepts are discussed in greater detail below.

Events that make information public

A published document, the availability for sale of a product, a demonstration of a machine or process—anything which imparts information becomes part of the state of the art. Separate communications can only be combined (known as 'mosaicing') if they refer to each other. Clearly the publication of a patent application or academic article makes information public. The law on this is strict; what matters is that people *could* access the information.

Novelty

✳✳✳✳✳✳✳✳✳

Figure 7.3 For an invention to be old

Information must have been communicated to the public

the public means anyone who was free to pass the information on

Before the priority date of the invention

The information must have (as at its date of publication)

disclosed (ie set out) the invention to the skilled person

enabled the skilled person to carry out the invention

'The invention' means anything falling within the scope of a claim (each claim in a patent is treated separately)

Research Corporation/Publication (T381/87) [1989] EPOR 138

FACTS: A scientific paper was placed on the shelves of a library to which members of an academic society had unrestricted access.

HELD: It became public when it was placed on the shelves. The question of whether anyone (let alone a skilled person) actually read it that day (or ever) was not relevant.

It was important that members could tell the world about what they read. If membership imposed a duty of confidence, the patent would have been valid.

In *Lux Traffic Control Systems Ltd v Pike* [1993], traffic signals used on a public road made public information that could be gleaned by observing how they operated.

For some potential information-disclosing events, duties of confidence may arise and mean that there is no disclosure—consider disclosures of products to potential suppliers and customers and apply the principles from Chapter 6. The confidentiality status of personal communications also needs to be carefully considered.

Disclosure of the invention

The House of Lords addressed the issue of disclosure in *Synthon*.

Synthon BV v SmithKline Beecham [2005] UKHL 59

FACTS: Similar to *Mobil* (see 'Novelty of products, processes, and uses'), the prior art, if followed, would have resulted in the invention, but did not say (and it would not have been clear) that the invention would result.

> **HELD:** Novelty involves two questions—there must be a disclosure and it must be enabling: but a 'disclosure' means 'disclosure of the invention', which this prior art did not do because the invention did not inevitably result from following it.

This over-loading of meaning on the word 'disclose' can confuse. The TBA in *Mobil* stated the same thing more clearly: 'The word "available" carries with it the idea that, for lack of novelty to be found, all the technical features of the claimed invention in combination must have been communicated to the public, or laid open for inspection.'

The concept of enablement

In addition to being public and disclosing the invention, a piece of prior art must enable the invention to destroy its novelty.

Disclosure of a chemical compound without a recipe that a skilled chemist could follow to make it will not generally make that chemical available to the public (see also *Asahi*, discussed in 'Applications forming part of the state of the art when they are filed').

Availability to the public (G01/92) [1993] EPOR 241

FACTS: The application was for a chemical compound.

HELD: Where it is possible for the skilled person to discover the composition or the internal structure of the product and to reproduce it *without undue burden*, then both the product and its composition or internal structure become state of the art. The skilled person can make use of their general technical knowledge in doing this.

Protection for inventors against certain disclosures

Where a disclosure is made within the period of six months prior to the priority date of an application in one of the following situations, the novelty of the invention claimed is not affected by it (s 2(4)). The situations are:

- disclosures by people in breach of a duty of confidence owed to the inventor, or in consequence of such a disclosure;

- disclosures resulting from the inventor displaying the invention at an international exhibition.

Novelty of products, processes, and uses

A new product is, by definition, novel. But a patent can be obtained for a new process, and that process may consist of a new way of using or making a known product. In the area of pharmaceuticals, **EPC, Art 54(4) and (5) and PA 1977, s 4A(3) and (4)** state that where a new

Novelty

✱✱✱✱✱✱✱✱✱✱

pharmaceutical use is discovered for an already known chemical composition, a claim to the composition 'when used' in the newly discovered treatment will be new. This principle extends to further pharmaceutical uses found for a product already known to have some pharmaceutical use(s).

Abbott Respiratory/Dosage regime G2/08 [2010] EPOR 26 (EPA)

HELD: Where the use of a chemical to treat an illness was known, it was possible to patent a particular new dosage regime for treating that illness with that chemical; but the new regime must reflect a previously unknown technical effect (**Mobil** principles). The previous practice of framing such claims in 'Swiss-type' form is no longer accepted.

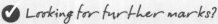 ✅ Looking for further marks?

Such claims can be used to 'evergreen' protection where pharmaceutical patents are reaching the end of their lives. This practice is controversial in the EU and other jurisdictions and involves competition law issues—see Shadowen, Leffler, and Lukens, 'Bringing Market Discipline to Pharmaceutical Product Reformulations' (2011) 42(6) IIC 698–725.

A similar principle is applied to non-pharmaceutical substances. In *Mobil/Friction reducing additive* [1990], the TBA held that a technical effect is not made available if it 'remains hidden or unclear' and this is a question of fact in each case. Claims to a use of a substance for the purposes of achieving a technical effect will be novel if the technical effect was not available. This approach has been followed by the Court of Appeal in *Actavis v Merck* (discussed in 'Relationship between national laws, the Convention, and the EPO').

Sometimes a patent discloses an invention where one element of the claim is not a particular thing, but a group of things—this is common in chemical claims, where the invention may just require 'an organic solvent' and possibly give a list of alternatives. A later inventor may discover that a particular solvent works better, or in particular contexts where others do not. 'Selection patents' are granted for such inventions. The earlier UK doctrinal basis for doing so was unclear, but application of *Mobil* principles naturally achieves a sensible outcome:

Bayer Diastereomers (T12/81) [1979–85] EPOR B308

HELD: If a technical property of one particular member of a group is the basis of the invention, and that technical property was not known to the public, then there is novelty.

Dr Reddy's Laboratories (UK) Ltd v Eli Lilly & Co Ltd [2009] EWCA Civ 1362, [2010] RPC 9

HELD: *Bayer* should be applied in selection patent cases.

Applications forming part of the state of the art when they are filed

PA 1977, s 2(3) provides that where a first patent application (A) is published (anywhere in the world) on or after the priority date of a second application (B), but the priority date of application A is before the priority date of application B, material in application A forms part of the state of the art for application B. See 'Claiming priority from an earlier application' for an explanation of the priority date.

Asahi KKK's Application [1991] RPC 485 (HL)

Something is in the prior art for the purposes of **s 2(3)** provided:

- the material was in both application A and its priority document;
- that material constitutes an enabling disclosure of the invention claimed in application B.

This is not clear from the wording of s 2(3) or s 5 (which deals with priority), but was clarified in *Asahi*. This interpretation is necessary to avoid 'double patenting', where two applications filed at or around the same time are both granted and their claims overlap—an undesirable result.

Inventive step/non-obviousness

To be non-obvious, an invention must differ from the prior art in more than minor details. Obviousness is judged from the point of view of the skilled person: would the invention have been obvious to them at the priority date? In *Pozzoli SpA v BDMO SA* [2007], the Court of Appeal re-formulated its decision in the earlier *Windsurfing* [1985] case as follows:

(1) (a) Identify the notional 'person skilled in the art';

    (b) Identify the relevant common general knowledge of that person;

(2) Identify the inventive concept of the claim in question or if that cannot readily be done, construe it;

(3) Identify what, if any, differences exist between the matter cited as forming part of the 'state of the art' and the inventive concept of the claim or the claim as construed;

(4) Viewed without any knowledge of the alleged invention as claimed, do those differences constitute steps which would have been obvious to the person skilled in the art or do they require any degree of invention?

The EPO has developed the 'problem-and-solution approach' or PAS:

- identifying the closest or most relevant piece of prior art;
- determining the technical problem that the claimed invention addresses and successfully solves; and

Inventive step/non-obviousness

✱✱✱✱✱✱✱✱✱✱

- examining whether or not the claimed solution to the objective technical problem is obvious for the skilled person in view of the state of the art in general.

The UK courts have acknowledged PAS:

> **Actavis UK Ltd v Novartis AG [2010] EWCA Civ 82, [2010] FSR 18**
>
> **HELD:** Much of the **Pozzoli** approach simply correctly orients the court. Step 2 is only useful if there is agreement on what the inventive concept was (otherwise it could involve pre-judging the question). The key element of the test was step 4. As to that, the problem-and-solution approach was sometimes useful, but probably more useful to a patent examiner than a court undertaking a full enquiry, where many evidential factors might come into play. The central question is: 'Was the invention obvious to the skilled person?'

Particular inventive step issues

Non-technical inventions

> **Esswein/Automatic Programmer (T579/88) [1991] EPOR 120**
>
> **HELD:** Inventiveness must be of a technical nature, not in the recognition of a market opportunity the realization of which was technically obvious (in this case, a washing machine with only two programmes).

The UK courts adopt a similar approach, though with a different concept of what 'technical' is (see 'The excluded categories').

The 'obvious-to-try' difficulty

> **Conor Medsystems Inc v Angiotech Pharmaceuticals Inc [2008] UKHL 49**
>
> **HELD:** If a claimed solution to a problem was in fact easily achievable, but there was not a fair expectation that it would work technically, the invention is not obvious. This applies even if the claimed solution does not in fact solve the problem—but in such cases the claim may fail for insufficiency (see 'Sufficiency, scope of claims, and priority').

Invention vs investment

> **Biogen v Medeva [1997] RPC 1 (HL)**
>
> **FACTS:** A large team of post-doctoral researchers spent a long time developing a product in the field of biotechnology.
>
> **HELD:** That alone did not imply inventiveness; an inventive step must still be identified.

Long-felt want

Inventors often rely on the fact that there had been a 'long-felt want' for a solution to the problem, to support their claims of non-obviousness. These arguments do not determine the question, as there may be non-technical reasons why the invention was not thought of earlier.

Sufficiency, scope of claims, and priority

These topics relate to the relationship between the description of the invention in the **specification** and the breadth and the content of the claims. There are two separate issues:

- Does the description properly teach how to put the invention into effect (known as sufficiency or **teaching**, required by **PA 1977, s 14(3)/EPC, Art 83**)?
- Are the claims too broadly drafted—do they claim too much, bearing in mind what is disclosed (is there 'support' for the claims, required by s **14(5)/Art 84**)?

Teaching

PA 1977, s 14(3) and **EPC, Art 84** require the invention to be taught 'clearly and completely enough for it to be performed by a person skilled in the art' (ie the skilled person). This is judged at the date of the publication of the application.

> **Exxon/Fuel Oils (T409/91)** *Eli Lilly & Co v Human Genome Sciences Inc* [2011] UKSC 51
>
> **HELD:** Teaching requires that the skilled person can, without undue burden, and without carrying out a research programme, put the invention into effect across the breadth of the claim using only common general knowledge.

Support/scope of claims

In *Asahi* and *Biogen*, the House of Lords held that 'support' in the Act requires teaching. This, and the *Exxon* doctrine, were approved by the House of Lords in *Lundbeck*.

> **Generics v Lundbeck** [2009] UKHL 12, [2009] RPC 13
>
> **HELD:** That for teaching:
>
> - of process claims, the claims must not be broader than the actual process disclosed in the description (so a whole class of processes, not all of which are taught, cannot be claimed). In this they upheld the earlier decision in *Biogen*;
> - of product claims, it is enough to teach one way of making a product falling within the scope of the claims (clarifying an issue that *Biogen* had left open).

The House regarded this as being consistent with the proposition that the scope of the monopoly granted should correspond to the technical contribution to the art made by the invention, but not necessarily be limited to the precise disclosure made.

Claiming priority from an earlier application

Under the terms of the **Paris Convention**, where an inventor files an application in one country for an invention, they may, within one year, file applications for the same invention in other countries that will have the priority date of the earlier application. The **EPC** allows priority to be claimed, in addition, from an earlier EPO application. This provision is extremely important to inventors:

- Worldwide priority can be achieved without making multiple applications.

- The application from which priority is claimed can be an informal document—it does not need to comply with all the formalities necessary for an application to proceed to grant.

- The 'Convention Year' can be used to obtain funding or assess the commercial viability of the invention before investing the considerable sums required for international protection, and to hire a patent agent to draft an application that does comply with all the formalities and supervise worldwide applications if needed.

For a claim to priority to succeed, the priority document must disclose sufficient information. **EPC, Art 87** requires it to be for the 'same invention' as the subsequent application; **PA 1977, s 5(2)(a)** states that the claims of the application must be 'supported' by the priority document.

Reference by the President of the EPO/Requirement for claiming priority of the 'same invention' (G2/98)

HELD: This requirement means that the invention must be disclosed in an enabling manner in the priority document.

UnilinBeheer NV v Berry Floor NV **[2004] EWCA Civ 1021**

HELD: It was unhelpful that the exact words of the Convention had not been used in the Act, but that the best approach was to follow the wording of the Convention and *G2/98*.

The requirement that the priority document enables the invention, when combined with the rules on novelty for priority documents (see 'Applications forming part of the state of the art when they are filed'), ensures that 'double patenting' should not occur. See Figure 7.4.

Figure 7.4 Claiming priority, and internal validity

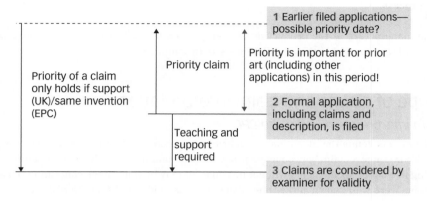

Ownership and duration of patents

Anyone can apply for a patent, but only the inventor or someone claiming rights from the inventor can be granted a patent from the application. This is not silly; when staking a claim to priority in a technologically competitive environment, days can be important. The system allows a claim to be made as soon as possible, with ownership issues being sorted out later.

University of Southampton's Applications [2006] EWCA Civ 145

HELD: The inventor is the person or people responsible for the inventive concept, who had contributed the 'heart' of the invention.

This will not necessarily be the investor, or all the researchers who would be named as co-authors of any resulting academic paper.

Patents last for 20 years from the date of filing of the application. This is the date from which damages can be claimed should any patent be granted, but a claim cannot actually be made until grant.

(EU law provides for 'supplementary protection certificates' to extend patent protection in the case of pharmaceutical products where obtaining regulatory approval has delayed the time to market.)

Infringement of patents

For a patent to be infringed, it is necessary that:

- a product or process falls within the scope of a claim of a patent;

- a person commits an infringing act within the jurisdiction in relation to that product or process.

The manufacture of the product or the carrying-on of the process does not necessarily have to take place within the jurisdiction—see 'Infringing acts'.

Scope of claims and claim interpretation

Claim interpretation under the EPC

Patent claims define the invention by describing a number of features of a product or process. To infringe a claim, a product or process must contain every element. Something containing five out of six elements will not infringe—it may be that things containing those five elements were well known at the time of the invention and it is the addition of the sixth that was new.

The precise technological scope of a patent is affected by how the words of the claims are interpreted. Approaches to claim interpretation lie between two extremes: strict reliance on the claim wording; and the interpretation of the scope of the monopoly on the basis of the specification as a whole, with the claim wording being a guide.

EPC, Art 69 deals with infringement, and its protocol says that the correct approach lies somewhere in between the two: the claims are important but should be interpreted in a way that takes into account the patent as a whole. The EPO does not deal with infringement issues, so there are no decisions from it that help to interpret Art 69. Accordingly, approaches to claim interpretation remained diverse within Europe, with each country to an extent continuing with its pre-EPC doctrine. There were two approaches, exemplified by the UK and Germany:

- The UK approach started from the basis of the wording of the claims and then sought to interpret that (known as 'purposive construction').
- The German approach considered the patent as a whole when considering its scope, which would include things that were technically equivalent to the invention set out in the patent (the 'doctrine of equivalents').

When the EPC 2000 was drafted, the protocol to Art 69 was amended by adding the following article:

Article 2 Equivalents

For the purpose of determining the extent of protection conferred by a European patent, due account shall be taken of any element which is equivalent to an element specified in the claims.

This requires the consideration of technical equivalents at the level of the elements in a claim: to infringe, something must contain all the elements of the claim, but technically equivalent features *may* be considered as providing those elements.

UK claim interpretation cases

The **PA 1977** says nothing about claim interpretation, and **Art 69** is one of the articles specified in s **130(7)**, so **Art 69** and its protocol should be followed. In *Improver*, the court adopted a test based on the **Patents Act 1949** law, though calling them the 'protocol questions':

Improver Corp v Remington Consumer Products Ltd [1990] FSR 181

The questions to ask are shown in Figure 7.5.

Many commentators expressed doubts that this properly accorded with the Convention. The House of Lords has responded to the doubts and to the introduction of the **EPC 2000** by relegating the importance of the *Improver* test.

Figure 7.5 *Improver Corp v Remington Consumer Products Ltd* [1990]

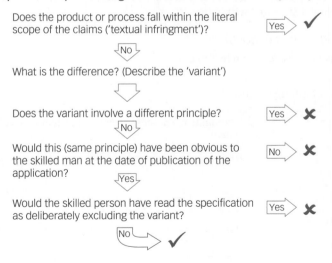

Infringement of patents
✳✳✳✳✳✳✳✳✳✳✳

Kirin-Amgen v Transkaryotic Therapies [2004] UKHL 46, [2005] RPC 9

FACTS: The invention involved biotechnology and the contentious words of the claim had no ordinary language meaning.

HELD:

- The *Improver* approach remained a useful approach in cases where the meaning of an ordinary word or phrase required interpretation.
- It was not useful where, as here, technical terms had no meaning other than to a skilled person. The meaning in context of the terms (as to which expert evidence is needed) defines the scope of the claim.
- The overriding task was to provide a fair measure of protection to the patentee, while providing certainty for others reading the patent and trying not to infringe it, in accordance with **Art 69** and its protocol.

Infringing acts

The **EPC** specifies how patents can be infringed in general terms; the provisions of the **PA 1977** are contained in s **60** and are set out in the following sections. Only acts taking place within the UK can infringe. But where products are made elsewhere, or a process is carried on elsewhere, infringement may occur when the products or products of the process are imported into and distributed within the UK.

Direct infringing acts (s 60(1))

Direct infringing acts are shown in Table 7.1.

Table 7.1 Direct infringing acts

Process claims	(Products of) process claims	Product claims
Using the process	Disposing of	Making, disposing of
Offering the process for use in the UK		Offering to dispose of
	Using or importing	Using or importing
	Keeping for disposal or otherwise	Keeping for disposal or otherwise
With knowledge that use would infringe (s 60(1)(b))	Any product obtained directly by means of the process	A product falling within the claim

Indirect infringement under s 60(2)

It is an infringement for a person to supply or offer to supply the 'means, relating to an essential element of the invention, for putting the invention into effect when he knows, or it is obvious to a reasonable person in the circumstances, that those means are suitable for putting, and are intended to put, the invention into effect'. There is an exception where what is supplied is a 'staple commercial product'.

This protects against a patent being evaded by selling a kit of parts for a patented product, or a product with an element missing, which can easily be obtained separately. As an element of the claim would be missing, there would be no infringement under s 60(1); and the rules of claim interpretation cannot extend a claim to cover something that is missing a required element. Indirect infringement deals with this problem.

Defences to patent infringement

A patent is only infringed if the infringing activity is done without the consent of the proprietor. So sub-contractors acting on the precise instructions of the patent owner have that permission. Consent can also be implied, for example when a machine that carries out an infringing process is sold by the proprietor of the process patent.

PA 1977, s 60(5) contains a number of defences:

- Activities that are both private and non-commercial do not infringe.

- Acts for experimental purposes where the purpose of the experiment is to investigate the technology of the patent do not infringe.

Monsanto Co v Stauffer Chemical Co [1985] RPC 515

FACTS: Experiments into a drug were carried out for the purposes of obtaining regulatory approval.

HELD: The defence did not apply, as the research was not to investigate the technology. Note: there are separate defences related to the regulatory approval of patented pharmaceuticals that are beyond the scope of this book.

Market-related research would not fall within this defence.

- Pharmacists may prepare a pharmaceutical composition in response to a prescription without infringing a patent.

- Farmers may keep seeds for propagation and breed animals without infringing any patent if they obtained the original seeds or livestock from the patent owner. (In practice, patented material of this sort is supplied in sterile forms that cannot reproduce.)

- There are defences that apply to things temporarily within the jurisdiction on aircraft and ships.

Revocation, invalidity, and amendment

****

Where a defendant can show that a patent is invalid, s 74(1)(a) says that it is a defence to a claim for patent infringement. A counterclaim for revocation does not have to be made when this defence is put forward, but it often is.

Where a defendant feels that their product or process is no different (from a technological perspective) from an item of prior art, they can raise the '*Gillette* defence'.

Gillette v Anglo-American Trading (1913) 30 RPC 465

HELD: A defendant may simply state that their product/process is not novel. This implies the argument that 'if the claimant says their claim is so broad as to cover me, it must be invalid; alternatively if their claim is not that broad, I don't infringe'. The defendant does not have to say whether they are arguing for invalidity or non-infringement—they must simply show that what they are doing is the same as the prior art.

There is a defence to claims for damages (not to an injunction) in s 62 where the defendant can show that they did not know and had no reason to believe that the patent existed. Proprietors mark their products with the patent numbers that apply to them in order to deal with this situation: s 62 states that merely stating that a product is patented is not sufficient to provide the necessary knowledge.

Where the defendant can show that they were carrying on the allegedly infringing activity before the publication of the patent application, they may continue those activities (s 64). The defence does not limit the amount of activity, but the defence is limited to the technical scope of the prior activity. 'Serious preparations' for an activity also trigger the defence.

Revocation, invalidity, and amendment

Anyone may oppose a patent on the grounds set out in PA 1977, s 72. These include all the main requirements for grant of a patent (novelty, obviousness, patentable subject matter, and lack of teaching). They do not include that the claims are not supported—but the courts have interpreted that as involving teaching, so it is possible to oppose a patent on the basis that the claims are too wide. A patent cannot be opposed on the more formal requirements that would have applied at the time of grant.

An opponent may apply to the court or the patent office for revocation of a patent, or in a counterclaim to infringement proceedings brought against them.

The action for groundless threats

There are similar actions in respect of design right, registered trade marks, and registered designs (UK and EU). The purpose is to remedy a particular scenario of abuse. Only those with a high level of commitment and investment in a product would think it worthwhile litigating over it, whether as a claimant or defendant: there are costs and risks involved. A rights owner may take advantage of this by not suing the manufacturer or importer of possibly infringing articles (they may defend strongly and counterclaim for revocation). Instead, they will go after distributors and sellers of the product, who may prefer to cease stocking the product rather than litigate. This could have the result of snuffing out the competition from the allegedly infringing product while avoiding litigation.

The action for threats in PA 1977, s 70 ensures that if this occurs, the rights owner can take action against the threats issuer, effectively forcing them to put their money where their mouth is. The scope and limitations to the action reflect this objective:

- The action need not be taken by the person threatened—the normal scenario is that a manufacturer takes action in respect of threats made to a distributor or seller.

- The threat must be a threat of legal proceedings, but that is interpreted functionally by the courts: if an ordinary business person receiving the communication would take it as a threat, it is a threat.

- Threats against manufacturers or importers of products are not actionable, or threats limited to accusations of manufacturing or importing.

- It is a defence to the action to show that the person threatened was indeed infringing.

Exploitation, dealings, and remedies

A patent application is an item of property that can be assigned and licensed, as can a patent once granted. Patents can also be mortgaged. The PA 1977 requires assignments to be in writing and registered at the patent office: if an assignment has not been registered, the assignee may not be granted a remedy in an infringement claim.

Before a patent is applied for, rights in a prospective invention can be dealt with as trade secrets—see Chapter 6.

The terms that can be included in patent licences are restricted by competition law, which is beyond the scope of this book.

 Key cases

Case	Facts	Principle
UnilinBeheer v Berry Floor [2007] EWCA Civ 364n, [2007] FSR 25	A European patent for clip-together flooring systems was the subject of an opposition (started within the nine-month opposition period) at the EPO. The UK part of the patent was litigated and held to be valid and infringed. Subsequently the EPO upheld the opposition.	The EPC is a compromise between keeping all power at state level and devolving it to the EPO. Illogical results flow from this. The court cannot bend its rules as to the final nature of judgments so as to create a more sensible system. That can only be achieved at a diplomatic level by the development of an enhanced system.

Key cases

✱✱✱✱✱✱✱✱✱✱

Case	Facts	Principle
	The UK court did not reverse its earlier decision on infringement; the defendant remained liable for damages.	
PBS Partnership/ Controlling Pension Benefits System (T931/95) [2002] EPOR 52	The patent applied for contained various claims relating to a method of computing pensions benefits using a computer, and apparatus for implementing it. The method could be implemented by programming a computer using known techniques and the application did not teach any specific programming technique.	The claims were not excluded as they involved a piece of hardware (a computer), which is of a technical nature, or the use of it. They did not, therefore, cover excluded matter as such. Any novelty and inventive step in the claims was limited to the fields of pensions calculation and computer programming. These areas did not involve any technical input, so inventiveness in them did not count towards inventive step. The claims were refused for lack of inventive step.
Symbian Ltd v Comptroller General of Patents [2008] EWCA Civ 1066, [2009] RPC 1	The invention concerned a particular way of organizing the structure of 'library' programs. These are files containing computer code that can be used by unrelated programs running on the same computer. The performance and usefulness of the computer depends on this structure—the Symbian structure was claimed to avoid the need to reinstall dependent applications when the library was updated.	The 'contribution approach' set out in *Aerotel* was applied. In this case, the contribution to the art was a computer system that functioned in a particular way. It was not simply a program, as the effectiveness of the method depended on the **technical characteristics** of the computer on which the programs ran (eg the way memory is addressed by the processor). Note: the result would almost certainly have been the same if the 'any hardware' approach was applied, as the inventive step would not be confined to the non-technical arts of programming, but would involve considerations of computer technology.
Lux Traffic Control Systems Ltd v Pike [1993] RPC 107	Prototype traffic lights were tested on a public road. Some information could be gleaned from noting the manner of operation of the lights by observing their operation. More information could be gleaned by opening a cover on the equipment and examining the adjustments available, but the cover was locked.	The information from merely observing was available to the public. The information that required opening the machine was not available, as it could only be obtained by interfering with the lock. Note: the foreman with access to the key to the cover had been placed under a duty of confidence.

Case	Facts	Principle
Mobil/Friction reducing additive (G02/08) [1990] EPOR 73	The claim was for an engine oil additive. It was known to reduce corrosion, but the patent claimed use of the additive as a friction-reducing agent. The friction-reducing properties of the additive were not previously known to the public.	Where a *technical effect* arises automatically when a substance is used, it is a question of fact whether the effect is made available to the public. In this case, the friction-reducing properties of the additive were not made available by the prior knowledge of the additive's properties. A claim to 'Use of [the substance] as a friction-reducing additive' was new.
Pozzoli SpA v BDMO SA [2007] EWCA Civ 588, [2007] FSR 37	The invention concerned a CD case in which many CDs were stacked in overlapping stepped fashion that enabled them to be separately clipped in via their central holes. Both the principle of overlapping discs and the manner of clipping-in were known. There was 'prejudice' in the field to overlapping discs without protection between them to avoid surface damage.	The **Windsurfing** test was re-formulated (see 'Inventive step/non-obviousness'). The inventive concept was not the same thing as the problem to be solved—here it was just the idea of combining stepped overlapping with known clipping-in means. The fact that some were averse to this solution because of the lack of protection for the discs did not mean that there was an inventive step. It was obvious to do it even if, prior to the claimants, people chose not to do so.

🗩 Key debates

Topic	Biotechnology patents and morality
Author	Amanda Warren-Jones
Standpoint	Summarizes the history of the development of the morality objections in the context of biotechnology patents. Current approaches to morality within the EU and globally are diverse. Warren-Jones argues that there is a need for a common approach to be developed worldwide, and that the EPO is in a position to do this, but in fact its judgments have induced confusion.
Source	'Finding a 'Common Morality Codex' for Biotech—A Question of Balance' (2008) 39(6) IIC 638–661
Author	Enrico Bonadio
Standpoint	Considers the implications of the Brüstle decision in this ongoing debate. The potential for a challenge to the EU under WTO rules is noted.
Source	'Biotech Patents and Morality after Brustle' (2012) 34(7) EIPR 433–443

Exam question

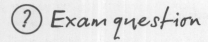

Problem question

Peter grows flowers on his allotment, where there is a small shed. Squirrels regularly nest in the roof of the shed. Last season Peter left a bag of parsnips hanging in the shed roof and then forgot about them. When he discovered the parsnips in the summer, he realized that the squirrels had left. As it happened, Peter's friend Dave had just told him that he had squirrel problems in the roof of his bungalow, so Peter took the bag of parsnips (by now dried) to Dave's bungalow and suggested to Dave's wife Jane (who opened the door) that the parsnips be put in the attic. Dave subsequently reported to Peter that the squirrels had left the attic. Peter did some research and discovered that a class of well-known anti-rodent chemicals (commonly called rodexins) includes one of the principal chemicals responsible for the smell of parsnips, and that the latter chemical (known as parsnipin) is available as a flavour additive. Peter conducted tests using various rodexins and parsnipin and his son's pet gerbils and found that parsnipin was a much more effective deterrent.

What are the prospects for Peter obtaining a patent for a rodent deterrent based on the parsnip flavouring?

See the Outline Answers section in the end matter for help with this question.

#8
Designs

Designs law is a collection of legal rights that can protect the design and appearance of products. In the UK, it comprises:

- copyright as it applies to infringement by making products;

- design right under **Part III of the Copyright, Designs and Patents Act 1988 (CDPA)**, an anti-copying right that lasts up to ten years from when products are first made;

- registered designs covering the UK, which may be obtained from the UK Intellectual Property Office (IPO), and registered designs covering the whole of the EU, which may be obtained from the European Intellectual Property Office (EUIPO). Registered designs provide a monopoly over making products with the same appearance as the design that has been registered, but design registrations are only valid if they are new and of distinctive character.

Designs law is not about any literary, musical, etc content recorded on a product—that will be protected by copyright in the straightforward way, as set out in Chapter 2. Similarly, the under-lying technological ideas may be protected by a patent.

Overview and history

In the UK, the applicability of copyright to protect designs for everyday objects has had a troubled history. Under the Copyright Act 1956, as interpreted by the courts, copyright in design drawings could be used to prevent designs for everyday, functional articles from being copied for the full copyright term. By contrast, copyright in design drawings for objects for which a design could be registered only lasted 15 years.

This position was clearly illogical and the CDPA sought to cure the problem by:

- restricting the scope of copyright protection to things that were artistic **works**;
- introducing 'design right' to provide a measure of protection to replace the lost copyright protection;
- extending the duration of registered designs to 25 years and making the requirements for registrability a little tighter.

Since then, registered designs law has been completely changed as a result of it being harmonized at EU level.

Design right questions

The law of industrial design is not an area that has generated great academic debate beyond the interpretation of the black-letter law. The problem for students is the number of different rights and the challenge of applying all those rights to any particular situation. But if you can do that accurately, you will do well in a designs law question. Table 8.1 at the end of this chapter will help to sort out which doctrinal concept relates to which right.

Copyright in designs

Copyright in designs works just like copyright as described in Chapter 2, so you may need to revisit that chapter. The following issues are particular to enforcing copyright within the design field, so are dealt with here, not in Chapter 2. The situation is summarized in Figure 8.1.

- A copyright **claim** must be established.
- The defence in CDPA, s 51 (the 's 51 defence') may mean that no remedy is available.

Establishing a copyright claim

A typical design dispute involves one manufacturer's products being allegedly copied by another. Let us say the products in question are plastic buckets. Copyright does not exist in mass-produced plastic buckets: they are not original (they are copies of the moulds from which they are made) and they are not artistic works (they do not fit into any of the categories

Figure 8.1 Copyright in designs for things

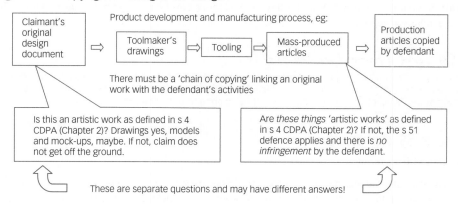

in **CDPA, s 4**). Yet a potential copyright claim may be made out by *identifying the original design document or model recording the design* and *proving a 'chain of copying'*. The elements of such a claim are set out in Figure 8.1.

Copying must be traceable through the production process as, in most cases, the original design documents will not be available and thus cannot be directly copied.

British Leyland Motor Corp Ltd v Armstrong Patents Co Ltd [1986] AC 577 (HL)

FACTS: The defendants copied BL car exhaust pipes, which were made from original design drawings, as replacement spare parts.

HELD: This was copying the drawings (so there would be infringement if a substantial part was taken).

This case provided urgency to the reform of designs law in the **CDPA**: though in this respect it remains good law, the **s 51** defence would now apply to exhaust pipes.

Design and manufacturing processes and the chain of copying

Most modern designers carry out their work on computers using design software such as Autocad®. This will produce documents that will be categorized as graphic works under **s 4** and be protected 'irrespective of artistic quality'. Instructions for computer-controlled machinery such as a milling machine or a 3-D printer can be generated from these drawings. That machinery can be used directly for production, or to make production moulds. There will be a chain of copying from the mass-produced products back to the drawings. In some cases designers will start by making a thing, a mock-up or model, which is reproduced in the production process (as was the case in *Hensher v Restawhile*—Chapter 2). That thing will be where any originality lies, so copyright will have to be asserted in it.

Copyright in designs

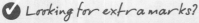

It is not certain such things will amount to artistic works (sculptures, works of artistic craftsmanship, or engravings). If they do not, there can be no copyright claim even if the end product is copied.

✔ Looking for extra marks?

Always check in what form the original designer expressed their design and deal explicitly with how it may be copied when considering a problem in this area. Make sure you consider copyright law fully (originality, taking of part, and so on) before moving on to the s 51 defence.

The s 51 defence

Section 51 is as follows:

(1) It is not an infringement of any copyright in a design document or model recording or embodying a design for anything other than an artistic work or a typeface to make an article to the design or to copy an article made to the design.

. . .

(3) In this section—

'design' means the design of the **shape** or **configuration** (whether internal or external) of the whole or part of an article, other than **surface decoration**; and
'design document' means any record of a design, whether in the form of a drawing, a written description, a photograph, data stored in a computer or otherwise.

The defence will apply only where three considerations are met:

- the design falls within the definition in s 51(3)—so designs for surface decoration are completely outside the scope of the defence;

Flashing Badge Co Ltd v Groves [2007] EWHC 1372 (Ch), [2007] FSR 36

FACTS: The claimant's products were shaped to fit the outline of a two-dimensional graphic applied to their surface.

HELD: This did not prevent that graphic (including its outline) amounting to surface decoration and thus being protected by copyright.

- the article whose design is recorded is not an artistic work—which means an artistic work as defined in s 4: bearing in mind the definition of 'design'; only those works that are created in three dimensions can be relevant here—that is, *sculptures, works of artistic craftsmanship*, and *engravings*. (Buildings are not articles, so architecture is outside the scope of the defence.) The Court of Appeal in *Lucasfilm* [2009] had held that the intention of the creator of the 'design document' is what matters when considering what it is a 'design for';

- the alleged infringement consists of making an article 'to the design'—considering the definition of design, the defence only covers the three-dimensional aspects of a copy. Printing a design drawing on a T-shirt will be copyright infringement in the usual way.

Thus, a design drawing for a plastic bucket is an artistic work (a graphic work) but the thing it is a 'design for' is not (it is not possible to argue that a plastic bucket is a sculpture). Plastic bucket manufacturers cannot, therefore, rely on copyright in their design drawings to stop their products' shapes being copied.

An example of a type of product that would be protectable by copyright is a garden gnome or similar item: in ordinary language we would describe the end product as a 'sculpture' and the law (see Chapter 2) would follow this.

Hi-Tech Autoparts Ltd v Towergate Two Ltd (No 2) [2002] FSR 254 (PCC)

Impressions from engraving plates are engravings. Thus the **s 51** defence will not be available to those who copy flattish articles (rubber car mats in the case of Hi-Tech) that can be said to be engravings.

Where the design is for something that is not flat enough to be an engraving, a measure of artistic intention will be needed for the article to be considered either a sculpture or work of artistic craftsmanship. This may be considered a loophole, and the law on engravings may change in the light of *Lucasfilm* (see Chapter 2).

Section 51 defence—issues

For copyright in 'surface decoration' to be enforced, it must be possible to separate the work on the surface decoration from the work on the aspects of shape and configuration to which the s 51 defence applies (*Lambretta Clothing Co Ltd v Teddy Smith (UK) Ltd* [2004]).

It is not clear if the defence applies where a three-dimensional article is illustrated in a drawing, but with no intention (at that stage) for it to be made (eg a cartoon character's vehicle). No case where this question is engaged has yet arisen, although the reliance on the intention of the author in *Lucasfilm* suggests that the defence will not be available.

Products on the borderline between art and design cause problems, as with copyright. The fact that the article is drawn first rather than made will mean that copyright exists in the drawings, but the status of the mass-produced product as art (or not) is still relevant when considering if the design is 'for an artistic work'.

Duration of copyright

For designs that are for artistic works, formerly **CDPA, s 52** had the effect that copyright can only be enforced for 25 years from the date on which articles first made to the design are marketed. **Section 52** was recently repealed by s 74 of the **Enterprise and Regulatory Reform Act 2013** in order to comply with the decision in *Flos*. The UK will be free to reinstate it once it leaves the EU, subject to any transitional arrangements.

Design right

****

Flos SpA v Semeraro Case e Famiglia SpA [2011] ECDR 8

FACTS: An Italian law restricted the enforceability of copyright in certain designs.

HELD: On a broad interpretation of the EU Directives and international conventions concerning copyright, this was contrary to EU law as it did not provide the protection required by (in particular) the **Information Society Directive**.

Where the defence does not apply because the design does not fall within the definition (eg designs for surface decoration), copyright is enforceable for the full term.

Design right

Design right is an anti-copying right that protects the shapes of articles. To avoid confusion, it is now often referred to as 'UK unregistered design right'.

Basic requirements

A design must be created in qualifying circumstances. The definition of 'design' is similar to that used in the s 51 defence—CDPA, s 213:

(1) Design right is a property right which subsists in accordance with this Part in an original design.

(2) In this Part 'design' means the design of ~~any aspect of~~ the shape or configuration (whether internal or external) of the whole or part of an article.

 . . . [Exclusions are set out]

(6) Design right does not subsist unless and until the design has been recorded in a design document or an article has been made to the design.

The reference to 'any part of an article' means that design right protects 'features of shape or configuration' rather than the article itself.

A Fulton Company Ltd v Totes Isotoner (UK) Ltd [2003] EWCA Civ 1514, [2004] RPC 16

HELD: A claimant asserting design right can choose which features of their design they put forward as qualifying for protection and being infringed.

The words 'any aspect of' were deleted from the statute on 1 October 2014. It is not clear what the effect of this deletion will be, but it may limit the scope for claimants to frame the description of their design in creative, abstract terms.

Of course, asserting design right in a single feature will not work, as the feature will fail the **originality** test—see 'Originality'.

Design right comes into existence as soon as a design document recording the design is created or an article is made to the design (s 213(6)). Thus, unlike the position with copyright, it does not matter how a design was created—any form of recording the design will suffice.

Shape and configuration of an article

These words date back to the pre-1988 legislation. Older cases held that 'shape' meant nothing more than 'configuration', but this has changed:

Mackie Designs Inc v Behringer Specialised Studio Equipment (UK) Ltd [1999] RPC 717 (HC)

HELD: The logical arrangement of electrical components in an electrical circuit amounted to 'configuration' but not 'shape'.

The mesh weave in *Bailey* (see 'A method or principle of construction') was either shape or configuration.

Originality

Section 213 states that designs are not original if they are 'commonplace in the design field in question'. This test applies to the design as asserted by the claimant; that is, a particular combination of features of shape and configuration.

Dyson Ltd v Qualtex (UK) Ltd [2006] held that:

- Originality is first assessed in the copyright sense of the word, then commonplace designs are eliminated. Simply taking two known designs and joining them together does not provide originality in the copyright sense, but combining a number of known design features might be original.

- Commonplace is not the same as well known; a product's appearance can become very well known, but its design features may not be commonplace if no or few other designs include those features. If a combination of features passes the originality test, the design as a whole will only be commonplace if that combination is commonplace.

In *Scholes Windows v Magnet* [2002], the Court of Appeal held that the other designs may be old designs, examples of which can still be seen, and do not necessarily have to exist in the UK if UK designers would be sufficiently aware of them. The law remains unclear as to how the boundaries of the 'design field in question' should be drawn, but in *Scholes* the design field was 'windows', whether of wood or uPVC.

Exclusions

Section 213(3) states that design right does not subsist in excluded things. If any features of shape or configuration are left after these things are excluded, then design right may be asserted in that set of features. In *Dyson*, it was held that any aspect of a design that was not excluded should be taken into consideration when deciding whether design right applied (ie when considering originality and not-commonplaceness), including minor features and features that were not visually significant.

Surface decoration

In *Dyson*, it was held that functional features could not amount to surface decoration, but that surface decoration could be built into the article when it was made and could consist of three-dimensional features. It is a question of degree whether non-functional shape features are decorations of a surface, or features of the shape itself.

Mark Wilkinson Furniture Ltd v Woodcraft Designs (Radcliffe) Ltd [1998] FSR 63

HELD: Grooves to highlight joins in a design for kitchen cabinets were 'surface decoration', while coarser features such as recessed door panels were not.

The 'must fit' exclusion

Section 213(3) states that design right does not subsist in:

(b) features of shape or configuration of an article which—

   (i) enable the article to be connected to, or placed in, around or against, another article so that either article may perform its function, or . . .

The intention of this was quite specific: to prevent monopolies arising over replacement spare parts, as in *BL v Armstrong* (see 'Establishing a copyright claim').

In *Dyson*, it was held that parts did not need to contact each other physically for the exclusion to apply. But the exclusion did not apply simply because articles needed to be placed in proximity to one another, even if there was not complete design freedom for the parts (because in use they must not get in each other's way).

The 'must match' exclusion

Section 213(3)(b) also excludes features that:

(i) are dependent upon the appearance of another article of which the article is intended by the designer to form an integral part, . . .

This exclusion was designed to deal with another spare-parts-related problem with the earlier law, exemplified by car body panels. A replacement panel must not only fit, but must match the shape of the whole car as originally designed. In *Dyson*, it was held that where it was not necessary to match (even though some customers might prefer a product exactly like the original), the exclusion did not apply.

A method or principle of construction

Methods or principles of construction are excluded. Though normally a method of construction would be achievable in a wide range of designs, in *Bailey v Haynes* this was not the case.

Bailey v Haynes [2007] FSR 10

FACTS: The article was a woven plastic mesh, the appearance of which followed from the type of weave.

HELD: This was a method of construction: in purposively construing the statute the court noted that allowing design right would prevent use of the method.

Ownership, qualification, and duration

The first **owner** of design right is (**s 215**):

- the commissioner, where the design is made pursuant to a commission;
- if not commissioned, the designer's employer if the design was created in the course of employment; or
- if neither of these apply, the designer.

Similar to copyright, if the designer is an EU national or resident, or if articles were first marketed in the EU, the design qualifies. Different from copyright, *the list of non-EU countries that count as qualifying countries is very small.* No international convention covers design right and most other countries have no equivalent legislation. You should assume that unless there is a relevant connection to the EU, design right does not apply to a design. This was the case in *Mackie*, where a US-originated design did not qualify for design right protection (and the copyright claim also failed).

The duration provisions are complex. Design right lasts:

- ten years from the date of first marketing articles made to the design; or
- at the end of the 15-year period from the date of initial creation of the design, if that is sooner; and
- in any case, 'licences of right' are available in the final five years of the term (the effect of this is that the owner can obtain financial compensation but cannot hold on to exclusivity in the design).

Infringement, defences, and remedies

Primary infringement

For **primary infringement**, design right is infringed by making, by a process of copying, articles 'exactly or substantially to the design'. It is also infringed by making a 'design document', but only if that is done for the purposes of manufacture of such articles (**s 226**).

In *L Woolley Jewellers Ltd v A & A Jewellery Ltd* [2002], the Court of Appeal held that the 'substantial part' test should not be applied to designs: copyright law on substantial taking flows from originality, and the originality requirement is modified in the case of design right: the statutory wording is different, indicating that Parliament did not intend the same test.

Note that there is no primary infringing act equivalent to s 18 (issuing): wherever an article comes from, a re-seller or importer can only be a secondary infringer.

Secondary infringement

For **secondary infringement**, a person infringes by importing or possessing for commercial purposes, selling or letting for hire, or offering or exposing for sale or hire an article which they knew or had reason to believe is an infringing article (s 227). An 'infringing article' is defined in s 228 in similar terms as for copyright infringement—see Chapter 2 on secondary infringement.

Defences and remedies

The usual remedies are available—damages or an account of profits, injunctions, and delivery-up or disposal of infringing articles. Additional damages may be awarded under s 229(3).

There are defences of lack of knowledge similar to those that apply in relation to performers' rights (ie somewhat more generous than those that apply to copyright):

- Primary infringers have a defence that they did not know, and had no reason to believe, that design right existed.

- There is an 'innocent acquisition' defence to an injunction for secondary infringers: where they lacked the knowledge required for secondary infringement when they acquired the articles, the only remedy against them is damages on a reasonable royalty basis.

Registered designs and the EU unregistered right

Registered designs provide a monopoly right that lasts 25 years for features of appearance of a product that are:

- new;

- give a different overall impression to the informed user;

- are not excluded—there is a 'dictated by technical function' exclusion, the 'must fit' exclusion, and a morality exclusion.

In 2001, the **Registered Designs Act 1949 (RDA)** was amended to implement **Directive 98/71/EC** on designs. This was, in fact, a ground-up re-write of the law. EU designs law talks of the 'appearance of products'. The concept of an 'article' and the concepts of 'shape and configuration' used in copyright and design right are not relevant to registered designs.

Revision tip

Ignore all pre-2001 cases in relation to registered designs. Old concepts such as 'eye appeal' and 'an article' are not relevant to the new law.

The legal structure of designs law in Europe

This structure is the same as that which applies in the case of trade marks. It is explained by means of Figure 1.1 in Chapter 1.

Because the substantive provisions of **Council Regulation (EC) No 6/2002 on Community Designs** and the Directive are identical, the law is only described once; it applies equally to EU registered designs and national registered designs.

Applying for a registered design

Before both the UK IPO and EUIPO, the applicant must submit a form with a representation of the design, typically either a drawing or a photograph, and the fee. Unlike patents, where all the requirements for patentability are examined, registered designs are not examined for **novelty** or individual character. Designs are examined to establish that:

- the application is for a 'design'—see 'The definition of a design—scope and exclusions';
- the design is not contrary to public policy or to accepted principles of morality;
- formal requirements are complied with.

Apart from this, it is up to opponents to challenge the validity of designs either of their own volition or in response to allegations of infringement. Applicants must assess whether the likelihood of a particular design registration being sustainable and of any use justifies the expense of obtaining and maintaining a registration.

UK applications are also examined to ensure that they do not include features dictated by technical function, or covered by the 'must fit' exclusion (**RDA, s 3A**). UK applicants can include disclaimers of excluded features in their application to forestall such an objection; otherwise the Registrar may declare the registration invalid or partially invalid.

The UK and EUIPO registers can be searched online and are well worth browsing.

Claiming priority

As with patents, it is possible to claim priority from an earlier design application when applying, meaning that novelty is judged as at the earlier date.

The period for making priority claims is just six months, pursuant to the **Paris Convention**.

The definition of a design—scope and exclusions

Design means:

- features of the appearance of a product (with special rules concerning parts of products);
- not including features dictated by technical function; and
- not including features falling within the 'must match' exclusion.

Registered designs and the EU unregistered right

✳✳✳✳✳✳✳✳✳✳

Features of appearance of a product

RDA, s 1(2) is as follows:

(2) In this Act 'design' means the appearance of the whole or a part of a product resulting from the features of, in particular, the lines, contours, colours, shape, texture or materials of the product or its ornamentation.

Registered designs can thus protect not only the shape of a product, but its surface decoration, or a combination of shape and surface decoration. They can also apply to designs that consist only of surface decoration—for example logos and symbols—provided they are applied to products (eg on packaging or labelling).

Apple Computer Inc v Design Registry [2002] FSR 38

FACTS: The designs were icons appearing on the display of a device.

HELD: These were registrable because they were built in at the time of manufacture.

It follows that icons forming part of software packages that are not built in to items of hardware are not registrable.

Note that the word 'appearance' means that internal features of a product that are not visible (without dismantling it) cannot be registered—unlike UK design right, where such features may be protected. See 'Registered designs and spare parts ("component parts of complex products")' for more in relation to this issue.

'Product' is defined as 'any industrial or handicraft item'. Illustrations in the content of books and magazines, art posters, etc are presumably not 'features of appearance of a product'. Logos, etc, which might adorn the cover of a book or magazine, would be. The dividing line between content and product is not yet clear.

Not solely dictated by technical function

Section 1C(1) states:

(1) A right in a registered design shall not subsist in features of appearance of a product which are solely dictated by the product's technical function.

The words 'solely dictated by ... technical function' have been interpreted to accord with the purpose of the exclusion, which is to prevent designs law creating monopolies over technology (which, if not patentable, should be free to use).

Lindner Recyclingtech GmbH v Franssons Verkstäder AB [2010] ECDR 1 (OHIM)

HELD: The correct approach was to exclude from protection those features of the design where technical function was the only consideration that determined the final shape.

The UK High Court approved this approach in *Dyson Ltd v Vax Ltd* [2010]. The question of whether there are other designs that could fulfil the technical function is not relevant: what matters is whether non-technical considerations played any part in that feature of the design.

The 'must fit' exclusion

Section 1C(2) states:

> (2) A right in a registered design shall not subsist in features of appearance of a product which must necessarily be reproduced in their exact form and dimensions so as to permit the product in which the design is incorporated or to which it is applied to be mechanically connected to, or placed in, around or against, another product so that either product may perform its function.

This is a more verbose version of the 'must fit' exclusion from design right protection and a similar approach will be taken by the UK courts pending an authoritative interpretation by the EUIPO or the ECJ. See 'The 'must fit' exclusion' in relation to design right.

Registered designs and spare parts ('component parts of complex products')

Designs can be registered for parts of products as well as whole products, but subject to strict limitations. **RDA, s 1(3)** defines 'complex product':

> a product which is composed of at least two replaceable component parts permitting disassembly and reassembly of the product; . . .

and the definition of 'product' includes 'a component part of a complex product'.

Section 1B(8) goes on to say that a design for such a component part will only be considered new and of **individual character** if the component remains visible in normal use of the whole product and to the extent that those visible parts are new and have individual character. 'Normal use' is defined as excluding maintenance or repair.

Presumably, the non-visible features will be ignored when considering infringement of any design, so the effect of this is that when considering registrability or infringement of a design for a component part, only the visible parts are relevant.

There is an exception to these limitations in s 1C(3): designs may be registered for components serving the purpose of allowing multiple assembly or connection of mutually interchangeable products within a modular system. This would apply, for example, to items of furniture that can be connected to form larger units, but which may also be used alone.

The replacement parts defence

Prior to the Directive, the treatment of spare parts under registered designs law varied. In the UK, for example, neither copyright, design right, nor a registered design could be used by an original product manufacturer to prevent the sale of replacement car body panels, while in Germany this was possible.

Registered designs and the EU unregistered right
✳✳✳✳✳✳✳✳✳✳

The EU could not agree on how to deal with this issue and therefore left it to the Member States by allowing, but not requiring, a defence for replacement spare parts. The UK has taken advantage of this in s 7A(5):

(5) The right in a registered design of a component part which may be used for the purpose of the repair of a complex product so as to restore its original appearance is not infringed by the use for that purpose of any design protected by the registration.

In *BMW v Round and Metal* [2012], the purpose was equated with the reason most users replaced the product.

Novelty

The key words of the statute are in RDA, s 1B(2):

a design is new if no identical design or no design whose features differ only in immaterial details has been made available to the public before the relevant date.

and by s 1B(5)(a) a design has been made available to the public if:

it has been published (whether following registration or otherwise), exhibited, used in trade or otherwise disclosed before that date.

As with patents, novelty is judged on a worldwide basis.

In the old UK law, **prior art** only counted if it involved the **industrial application** of a design. If the general principle is applied to the new law, things will only be prior art if they are industrial or handicraft items (products) with features of appearance, or representations of them in, for example, photographs or brochures. Illustrations of imaginary products would not count as *designs* at all; thus, it would be possible to register a design when a decision is taken to further exploit an artistic work by making merchandise.

In addition, the range of prior disclosures that do not count as prior art is much greater than is the case with patents. They are set out in s 1B(6) and cover:

- designs disclosed in breach of a duty of confidence; and designs disclosed 'as a result of an abuse in relation to the designer of any successor in title of his' within 12 months prior to the application date;

- designs that could not reasonably have become known 'in the normal course of business to persons carrying on business in the European Economic Area and specialising in the sector concerned';

- disclosures made by the designer within 12 months prior to the application date, or disclosures in that time consequential upon such disclosures.

While the first bullet point mirrors a similar protection for inventors in the case of patents, the second two points have no analogous protection in the case of patents and are of great practical importance.

The second point effectively rules out of consideration the type of one-off disclosure which, if discovered, can invalidate a patent. Disclosures in trade magazines, catalogues, etc, and products on general sale would still count as prior art. Some disclosures from outside the EU may be ruled out, although specialists in many business sectors would keep abreast of the world market as a matter of course.

The third point implements what is known as a 'grace period', during which the designer can publish without invalidating a later application. (Some jurisdictions have similar rules for patents, though not Europe!) It means that designers can perform product and market testing without having to impose conditions of confidence, and have 12 months to decide if the product is worth applying for a registered design. In any event, such disclosures may well not be notorious enough to get round the second point.

Although a design application must state the type of product involved (this helps in searching for prior registered designs), novelty must be across all product areas (and, similarly, the monopoly covers all product areas).

Green Lane Products Ltd v PMS International Group Ltd and others [2008] EWCA Civ 358, [2008] FSR 28

FACTS: A design of a spiky sphere was known and used as a massage ball, but subsequently used as a 'laundry ball'. An identical design was applied for designating the product as a 'laundry ball'.

HELD: The 'sector concerned' was held to be the sector of the prior art, not the sector of the product described on the application for registration. 'Persons carrying on business . . . and specialising' could include 'those who design, make, advertise, market, distribute and sell such products in the course of trade in the Community'. The massage balls prior art therefore meant that the design for laundry balls was not new.

Individual character

This requirement can be equated with the need for an inventive step in the case of patents: novelty is not enough, there must be meaningful distance from the prior art. By RDA, s 1B:

(3) . . . a design has individual character if the overall impression it produces on the informed user differs from the overall impression produced on such a user by any design which has been made available to the public before the relevant date.

(4) In determining the extent to which a design has individual character, the degree of freedom of the author in creating the design shall be taken into consideration.

In *Grupo Promer Mon Graphic SA v OHIM* [2012], the ECJ held that the 'informed user' was a customer for the products who was 'interested in the products concerned, [and] showed a relatively high degree of attention when using them'. Their knowledge lay somewhere between the average customer and a technical expert. The ECJ has also had to deal with competing design applications:

Celaya Emparanza y Galdos Internacional SA v Proyectos Integrales de Balizamientos SL (C-488/10) [2012] ECDR 17

HELD: Where two design applications cover competing designs, the second application will not have novelty and individual character if the first design is held to be valid.

The 'degree of freedom' point combines with the idea of the informed user to mean that small differences can be important. For example, all screwdrivers may look similar to someone with no interest in DIY. All screwdriver handles must be capable of being grasped securely—that imposes a design constraint. But the detailed features of the designs are not simply there for technical reasons. Within the constraints imposed by the nature of the product, designers try to make their products look good and work well. An informed user would recognize the differences of design.

In *Dyson v Vax*, it was held that the design freedom in question was the freedom of the designer of the product whose design was registered, assessed at the time of application. Expert evidence might help in deciding design freedom, but not when deciding overall impression, which the court could judge 'with its own eyes'.

Samsung Electronics (UK) v Apple Inc [2012] EWCA Civ 1339, [2013] FSR 9

FACTS: Two designs of tablet computer were necessarily similar because of the nature of the product.

HELD: S's product gave a different overall impression because the accumulation of details gave a different impression from A's clean, minimal design.

Ownership and duration

The ownership provisions for UK registered designs used to be the same as for design right—the creator, their employer, or the commissioner, or a successor in title. For EU designs, there is no commissioner rule (**Regulation 6/2002, Art 14**). Since 1 October 2014 the Commissioner rule no longer applies to UK designs (**RDA, s 2**).

Designs may be renewed in periods of five years, up to a maximum duration of 25 years from the date of application for registration.

There are no limitations in terms of nationality, residence, etc on who can apply, as required by the equal treatment provisions of the **Paris Convention, Art 2**.

Infringement and defences

Scope of designs covered

RDA, s 7(1) defines this as including the design as registered and

> any design which does not produce on the informed user a different overall impression.

Section 7(3) goes on to say that:

> In determining . . . whether a design produces a different overall impression on the informed user, the degree of freedom of the author in creating his design shall be taken into consideration.

These words are identical to those defining the distance a design must have from the prior art to be registered (novelty and individual character), save that the equivalent provisions of the Directive and Regulation use the phrase 'clearly different' in their recitals when talking about individual character, suggesting that a greater distance is required for the purposes of registration. However, it appears that this difference of wording was accidental, so the legal test that is used for individual character can be used when comparing the alleged infringement and the registered design for the purposes of infringement. (This was discussed in *Dyson v Vax*, which was an infringement case.)

You can therefore refer to the cases on validity and on infringement in relation to the 'individual character' test. The precise factual questions are different—for validity the design to be registered is compared to earlier designs, whereas for infringement the allegedly infringing design is compared to the design as registered.

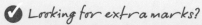 **Looking for extra marks?**

Be precise in what you are comparing with what when considering overall impression, and explain that the same test applies for infringement and validity of designs. As with patent questions, formulate the question for the 'informed user' precisely.

Effect of disclaimers

In the case of UK registered designs, the rights do not cover disclaimed features of a design or features excluded by a declaration of partial invalidity (s 7(4)—see 'Applying for a registered design'). Disclaimers are not possible in the case of EU registered designs—but any excluded features will be ignored when considering infringement issues (they do not fall within the scope of the design by definition).

Infringing acts

These are (s 7(2)):

(a) the making, offering, putting on the market, importing, exporting or using of a product in which the design is incorporated or to which it is applied; or

(b) stocking such a product for those purposes.

There is an 'exhaustion of rights' provision in s 7A(4):

> The right in a registered design is not infringed by an act which relates to a product in which any design protected by the registration is incorporated or to which it is applied if the product has been put on the market in the European Economic Area by the registered proprietor or with his consent.

Registered designs and the EU unregistered right
✳✳✳✳✳✳✳✳✳

This is, thus, a monopoly right, as the question of infringement is objective and does not require any intention or copying on the part of the infringer.

Defences

These are set out in s 7A(2)–(5). There are defences for:

- things done privately and for purposes that are not commercial;
- things done for experimental purposes;
- acts of reproduction for teaching purposes or for the purposes of making citations.

In the case of the last point, there must be a mention of the source of the design, and the act must be compatible with fair trade practice and must not unduly prejudice the normal exploitation of the design.

Remember the 'replacement spare parts' defence, dealt with earlier.

There are also defences for use on non-UK registered ships and aircraft temporarily present within the jurisdiction.

Litigation, challenges to validity, and threats

UK registered designs can be enforced and challenged through the UK court system, as you would expect. Applications for revocation can be made to the UK IPO.

In relation to EU registered designs, the Regulation allows Member States to designate some of their courts as 'Community Design Courts' of first instance, and courts of appeal from them. The UK has designated the courts that normally deal with intellectual property cases. These courts can:

- decide infringement issues (subject to EU jurisdictional rules that are beyond the scope of this book);
- give a declaration of invalidity of an EU registered design on application or if a counterclaim is made in infringement proceedings;
- decide a threats claim.

An EU registered design can also be challenged by applying to the EUIPO.

In all cases, the grounds for challenge are those described earlier for a design to be registered, including that the design includes matter that is excluded by the technical function or 'must fit' exclusions (s 11ZA).

In addition, designs can be challenged:

- by the owner of a copyright where the design is an unauthorized use of the work;
- by the owner of a 'distinctive sign' that has rights to prevent the use of the design (eg by rights in passing-off or a registered trade mark);

- by someone claiming to be the proprietor of the design as against the registered proprietor.

The first two points are important: prior intellectual property rights that conflict with the registered designs can be used to oppose the registration. Applicants must ensure that they obtain copyright, or sufficient rights under copyright, in the design before they apply.

Groundless threats of registered design infringement

The RDA provides for threats actions in respect of UK registered designs in s 26. Regulation 2 of the Community Design Regulations 2005 implements a threats action in respect of Community registered designs and the Community unregistered right. The Directive and the Regulation permit states to have such provisions.

These actions follow the form of the action in respect of patents—see Chapter 7.

Remedies

The usual remedies are available, including damages, injunctions, and delivery-up of infringing articles (**RDA, ss 24A–24D, Community Design Regulations 2005, regs 1A–1D**).

The Community unregistered right

The Community unregistered right is created by the Regulation. The right arises automatically and the conditions necessary for it to arise are the same as for a registered design to be valid, with the following differences:

- novelty and individual character are judged as at the first date on which the design is made available to the public (defined in **Art 11(2)**);
- the right is an anti-copying right, not a monopoly right;
- the right lasts three years from the date the design is first made available to the public within the EU.

This right will not provide sufficient protection for many designs, but it will provide protection while a registered design is being applied for and may be sufficient in the case of short-lived products.

Relationships between the different rights

According to **CDPA, s 236**, it is not an infringement of UK design right to do anything that would infringe copyright in a work that includes the design. The effect of this is that where there is a chance of a copyright claim (because the s 51 defence would not apply), claimants should claim copyright and design right in the alternative.

Beyond this, the rights can exist in parallel. In general, if the conditions for a registered design or the Community unregistered right are met just by the shape of a design,

Relationships between the different rights

✳✳✳✳✳✳✳✳✳✳

then design right is also likely to exist. But there are many designs where copyright cannot be enforced because of the s 51 defence, but where a design registration may be possible.

The conclusion is that where there is a possibility of a valid registered design being obtained, one should be applied for.

Table 8.1 shows how the different concepts relate to the different rights.

Table 8.1 Design rights: which doctrinal concepts apply?

Right issue	Copyright (bearing in mind s 51 defence)	UK unregistered design right	Registered designs (UK or EU)	EU unregistered right
Coverage: definition of 'design'	Shape and configuration of an article	Shape and configuration of an article	Appearance of a product	Appearance of a product
Originality or novelty required	Originality in design document or model	Originality in design, however created	Novelty—worldwide prior art with savings in **RDA**, **s 1B(6)**, same or different only in immaterial details	
Other requirements for protection	Design must be 'for an artistic work' (**s 51**)	Design must not be commonplace	Individual character, ie different overall impression on the informed user (customer who takes an interest)	
'Spare parts' special provisions?	No	No, but see 'must fit'	Yes—only visible parts of components protected, and in the UK and for EU designs further exclusions	
Materials and textures protected?	Not unless they are in the underlying drawing, etc	No	Yes	Yes
Surface decoration protected?	Yes	No	Yes	Yes
'Technical function' exclusion?	No	No—but 'must fit' will have some effect	Yes	Yes
'Must fit'—interfaces excluded?	No	Yes	Yes	Yes
'Must match' exclusion?	No	Yes	No	No

Anti-copying or monopoly right?	Anti-copying	Anti-copying	Monopoly	Anti-copying
Infringing things—how similar, etc	'Substantial part' as in copyright	Substantially similar—different from copyright	Not a different overall impression on the informed user (same test as for individual character)	
Duration	25 years from first marketing (now)/full copyright term (date to be fixed)	5–10 years' protection	25 years from application	3 years from first marketing
Commissioner, employer owns?	Employer rule only	Commissioner then employer rule	Employer rule only	Employer rule only

(✱) Key cases

Case	Facts	Principle
The s 51 defence		
***Lambretta Clothing Co Ltd v Teddy Smith (UK) Ltd* [2004] EWCA Civ 886, [2005] RPC 6**	The alleged design was a 1960s-style track top. Different plain-coloured fabrics were used for the panels forming the cut of the garment. The claimants asserted that the defendant, in copying their 'colourways' in its track top, had infringed design right or copyright.	The choice of colours was neither shape nor configuration, so design right did not apply. For copyright to be enforceable in surface decoration, the surface decoration had to be separately identifiable as a copyright work from the design document recording the shape and configuration. That was not the case here, so copyright could not be enforced in relation to the colourway. Note: applying copyright principles, the surface decoration does not need to be on a separate document, but the skill and labour in its creation must be separable.

Key cases

✳✳✳✳✳✳✳✳✳✳

Case	Facts	Principle
Lucasfilm v Ainsworth [2009] EWCA Civ 1328, [2010] Ch 503	The original designs for the storm troopers helmets in the *Star Wars* film were created in paintings and drawings. A made three-dimensional models of them, which were reproduced for use in the film. A subsequently made further reproductions of his models as collectors' items, without the consent of Lucasfilm, who owned copyright in the original drawings.	The creators of the original drawings had intended them to be used as props in the film: – the props for the film were not sculptures (see Chapter 2 for the definition of 'sculpture'); – the original drawings were not, therefore, 'designs for' artistic works (even though A's replica helmets were kept for display). The principle can be *inferred* that the intention of the creator of the design document as to how their design will be used, is important in deciding if it is a 'design for an artistic work'.
Design right		
Dyson Ltd v Qualtex (UK) Ltd [2006] EWCA Civ 166, [2006] RPC 31	The defendants made spare parts for the claimants' vacuum cleaners that not only fitted the claimants' products, but were visually similar to the claimants' spare parts. The claimants asserted design right in aspects of their spare parts designs. Some of these parts were copies of parts from earlier designs. There was some design freedom in the design of the shape of the spare parts. It was not necessary for the defendants to make similar-looking products for them to function.	The correct test for originality is to apply the copyright test, then consider commonplaceness. Parts consisting of a simple combination of copied parts failed the originality test. But a combination of known parts may be original. The 'must fit' exclusion does not require parts actually to touch. But it does not apply to design features that have to fit within a space without fouling nearby surfaces. The 'must match' exclusion only applied where the part *had* to be that shape (eg a replacement car body panel).
Scholes Windows v Magnet [2001] EWCA Civ 532, [2002] FSR 10	The claimants were the first to create sash windows in u-PVC. Many design features were commonplace in old designs of wooden sash windows, but not in contemporary window design (in wood or u-PVC). The claimants alleged design right infringement; the defence was that the design was commonplace.	Designs could be commonplace by being in use, even though products made to the designs were no longer produced. The design field should not be limited by the nature and purpose of the article, nor by the material. (But the court did not provide a positive test for what the design field was, other than that it depended on circumstances of each case.) In this case, the design field was 'windows', not 'u-PVC windows', so the designs were not original.

Case	Facts	Principle
L. Woolley Jewellers Ltd v A & A Jewellery Ltd [2002] EWCA Civ 1119, [2003] FSR 15	The defendant's jewellery pendants were similar in some respects to the claimant's. It was found that there had been copying of some features of the design. The first-instance judge had applied copyright principles to the question of infringement.	The correct test was not the same as for infringement. The test was to ask if the whole design of the defendants' product, including the copied elements, was substantially the same design as that in which the claimant asserted design right. It was possible that there would be copying of a substantial part by applying the copyright test, but not when applying the design right test.
	Registered designs	
Grupo Promer Mon Graphic SA v OHIM [2012] FSR 5 (ECJ)	The designs were 'pogs' or 'rappers', simple discs used to play a game. The designs included the shape of the edge of the disc and rings formed on the disc. The discs were used as promotional gifts with other products and played with by children.	The 'informed user' was a customer for the products who 'knew the various designs which existed in the sector concerned, possessed a certain degree of knowledge with regard to the features which those designs normally included and, being interested in the products concerned, showed a relatively high degree of attention when using them'. Their knowledge lay somewhere between the average customer and a technical expert. In this case, the informed user would include both children and marketing executives concerned with promotional gifts.
Dyson Ltd v Vax Ltd [2011] EWCA Civ 1206, [2012] FSR 4	The claimants had a registered design for the appearance of the whole of their vacuum cleaner, the design of many aspects of which involved technical considerations. The defendants' cleaner had some visual similarities, but was not identical. The claimants' cleaner looked 'smooth, curving and elegant', the defendants' 'rugged, angular and industrial'.	To be dictated solely by its technical function, there must be no reason for a design feature to be that shape, other than technical considerations. It was irrelevant whether other shapes could fulfil the technical function. In deciding individual character, the designs should be looked at overall, not minutely compared—here the impression was different.
Bayerische Motoren Werke AG v Round & Metal Ltd [2012] EWHC 2099 (Pat), [2013] FSR 18	D manufactured after-market alloy wheels for cars which were copies of BMW original designs, which were registered. Ordinary car users normally replace wheels for cosmetic purposes, not repair.	The words 'for the purposes of repair' in the derogation meant the ordinary purpose for which the component was replaced. Thus alloy wheels fell outside the spare parts defence.

Exam question

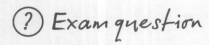

(?) Exam question

Problem question

Sarah is a tree surgeon. One weekend, she visited her parents with her chainsaw to cut down a tree in their garden. At her mother's suggestion, she fashioned some chairs, tables, and benches out of the trunk of the tree using her chainsaw. Sarah's parents run a garden centre and tearoom and they put the carved furniture on display, where it attracted great interest and the items sold for a high price. Recently, Sarah noticed cast concrete furniture, made by a Dutch company called Domen BV, on sale at her local garden centre. The Domen furniture looked very similar to her carved wooden furniture—there were chainsaw marks on the casting just like on Sarah's furniture. Sarah believes that the Domen furniture was made from casts taken from examples of her carved wooden furniture.

What rights does Sarah have in her carved furniture? Against whom can she take action, and will she be able to take any action against Domen in the Netherlands? What should she do to ensure the best protection?

See the Outline Answers section in the end matter for help with this question.

#9
Passing-off and trade marks

Key facts

- Passing-off is a common law cause of action, which protects traders against misrepresentations made by their competitors that confuse customers as to the source of **goods and services**. The typical passing-off scenario is where a first trader, by the use of a brand name, logo, slogan, or packaging, deceives customers into thinking that their products or services are associated with a second trader. If the second trader can prove that, and also prove loss, then they have a cause of action in passing-off. It must be proved that customer **confusion** has occurred, and this can be difficult.

- Registered trade marks provide traders with the opportunity to gain protection for their brand names and other brand identifiers, such as logos, packaging details, and slogans, by registering them as trade marks.

- While there are strict requirements for what can be registered as a trade mark, if a trader is able to register a mark, they will achieve better protection than from passing-off, as any use by another trader of the mark on the goods for which it is registered will infringe the trade mark and can be stopped.

- For this reason, traders should register trade marks wherever they can, rather than relying on passing-off to protect their brand identity.

Overview and history

The law of passing-off derives from the common law action for deceit; that is, the civil action for fraudulent misrepresentation. But passing-off now differs significantly from the law of deceit in that no intention to cause loss is required, and the misrepresentation can be completely innocent.

Registered trade marks were first introduced in the UK by the **Trade Marks Registration Act 1875**. Subsequent Acts extended the scope of what could be registered. The current Trade Marks Act is the **Trade Marks Act 1994 (TMA)**, which was brought in to implement **Directive 89/104/EEC** (now 2008/95/EC), known as the **Trade Marks Directive**. Registered trade marks can be obtained from the EUIPO pursuant to **Regulation 207/2009** ('the **Trade Marks Regulation**'). This is the same legal structure as for designs: see 'The EU registered rights (trade marks and designs)' in Chapter 1. On 23 March 2016, Regulation (EU) 2015/2424 came into force, making some significant amendments to the Trade Marks Regulation including re-naming 'Community Trade Marks' to 'European Union Trade Marks'. The Directive was similarly amended, and must be implemented by 14 January 2019. Given the likely timescale for the leaving the EU, the UK might not implement it. The changes will be noted in this chapter, but of course they apply to European Union Trade Marks, not UK trade marks. References to Article numbers are to those of the currently applicable Directive, 2008/95/EC.

As with other intellectual property rights, trade marks and the law of passing-off can be justified from a number of theoretical perspectives:

- The right to protect the name you trade under can be regarded as a fundamental right for all traders. In the modern marketplace, traders must be able to develop a brand for their products and services in order to attract the attention of consumers.

- The ability to distinguish products (in terms of where they originate) is important for the protection of consumers.

- Economic theory requires that for a market to work efficiently there must be accurate information for consumers so they can make informed decisions without the burden of high research costs.

Also, as with the other rights, a balance must be struck. If existing businesses were able to exclude others from too large an area of operation (in terms both of products and brand identifiers), that would constitute a barrier to entry into the market for competitors. The quality of information for consumers would be restricted, as it would become difficult to find out about new products.

Passing-off

The basic elements of the tort

The modern statement of the law is set out in the House of Lords case of *Reckitt & Colman v Borden* [1990]. This case set out the basic elements of the cause of action:

- the claimant has a protectable **goodwill**;

- the defendant makes a misrepresentation that is likely to deceive;
- that misrepresentation causes damage to the claimant's goodwill.

In most passing-off cases, the misrepresentation is that the defendant's products are either made by the claimant, or that they are in some way associated with the claimant, for example by licensing or quality control (though that is not always so: see 'Reverse passing-off').

Reckitt is notable for what it did not add to the law of passing-off. It confirmed that if the elements are made out, there will be passing-off—there are no exceptions. *Reckitt* had, by long use and skilful marketing, caused the public to associate a particular container **shape** with their product, so the fact that the container was **descriptive** did not matter.

In fact, there is only one defence to a claim of passing-off—where a defendant can show that they have developed their own goodwill associated with their use of the sign complained of (see 'Defence' below).

The need for UK-based goodwill

What is goodwill?

Many types of activity other than traditional businesses can acquire goodwill—including charitable organizations and campaigning/political organizations: trading activities are not needed.

Burge v Haycock [2001] EWCA Civ 900, [2002] RPC 28

FACTS: The Countryside Alliance were a campaigning organization.

HELD: They could bring an action because 'of the goodwill that they have established in the public eye for their activities which is, of course, a valuable property of theirs'.

The general definition of goodwill stems from Revenue case-law: 'the attractive force that brings customers to a business'.

My Kinda Bones v Dr Pepper's Stove Co [1984] FSR 289

FACTS: The claimant's restaurant had not opened, but had been advertised.

HELD: Provided marketing activity is carried on, that will provide sufficient connection with potential customers to generate *some* goodwill, even if trading has not started.

Passing-off

✱✱✱✱✱✱✱✱✱✱✱

However, there is no such thing as 'future goodwill'.

Teleworks Ltd v Telework Group Plc [2002] RPC 27

HELD: Where a company is expanding, it must rely on the goodwill it has at the time of the defendant's activities. Possible future activities are relevant, if at all, to the questions of misrepresentation and damage.

See later in this chapter as to misrepresentation and damage. Once trading activity has ceased, goodwill may continue but will decay:

Ad-Lib Club v Granville [1972] RPC 673

FACTS: An action was brought eight years after the original business closed.

HELD: Residual goodwill is a question of fact; in this case some goodwill remained.

Where is the goodwill located?

Passing-off is a tort that protects intangible property (goodwill). The English and Welsh courts will not accept passing-off claims concerning goodwill located outside the jurisdiction. Defining how connected to the jurisdiction activities need to be for goodwill to be located here is problematic.

The basic rule is that there must be 'customers in the jurisdiction'. This means in practice that:

- for businesses that sell products, the products must have been sold, or available for sale, to customers located in the jurisdiction (*Anheuser-Busch Inc v Budejovicky Budvar NP* [1984])—the source of the products would not be relevant (so overseas online sellers could develop goodwill);

- for businesses that provide services, the services must have been booked or ordered by customers when in the jurisdiction, even if the other party to the contract and the provision of the services were in a different jurisdiction (*Starbucks (HK) Ltd v British Sky Broadcasting Group Plc* [2015]).

Starbucks has authoritatively resolved some uncertainty on this issue in favour of the 'hard-line' approach applied in *Budweiser*: without customers in the UK there can be no action in passing-off, however well known a business is. It is clear from the earlier cases noted that these do not need to be paying customers.

A problem for international businesses is that they can achieve a high reputation in the UK, yet not be able to sue in passing-off because they do not trade here. It was possible for speculative businessmen to take advantage of this by setting up under an internationally known name and then demanding large sums of money for transferring the rights. **Article 6 bis of the Paris Convention and TMA, s 56** have curtailed the opportunities for this—see 'Blocking powers of holders of other rights'.

The misrepresentation
Ways of making a misrepresentation

The most common type of alleged passing-off is the use of a word or symbol on the packaging of a product, or in promotional or advertising material for a product or service. For a claimant to show that this amounts to a false representation they must show that the word or symbol they use is associated in the minds of the public with the claimant, or with their products or services.

Banal or descriptive words, phrases, or symbols are considered closely by the courts.

Phones 4u Ltd v Phone4u.co.uk Internet Ltd [2006] EWCA Civ 244, [2007] RPC 5

FACTS: The claimant asserted goodwill associated with 'Phones 4u'.

HELD: The test is whether the business was recognized by a substantial proportion of the public under that name. That was not the same as the test for whether the name could be registered as a trade mark (where there are special rules for descriptive names). The court considered the efforts made to publicize the name and evidence of 'brand awareness' and concluded this issue in favour of the claimant.

This requirement is separate from the requirement that the misrepresentation be effective (see 'Was the misrepresentation effective (did it confuse people)?'). If the defendant in *Phones 4u* had used a less similar name for its website, it might have succeeded in arguing that there was no confusion.

Misrepresentations can be implied; what matters is the perception by customers:

Associated Newspapers v Insert Media [1991] 1 WLR 571 (CA)

FACTS: Advertising 'flyers' were inserted in newspapers for delivery by a marketing company without the consent of the newspaper publisher.

HELD: This amounted to a misrepresentation that the publisher had chosen those flyers as being suitable for passing on to its readers.

A representation about what?

In the typical scenario, the representation concerns the source of the products or services, but misrepresentations can also involve:

- association with the claimant by means of licensing or endorsement, quality, or editorial control, as in *Associated Newspapers* (this can include character merchandising and celebrity endorsement activities);

Passing-off
✱✱✱✱✱✱✱✱✱✱

- the source of the defendant's products (so-called 'reverse passing-off'—see later in the chapter);
- the quality of 'genuine' products.

Colgate-Palmolive v Markwell Finance [1989] RPC 497 (CA)

FACTS: Genuine product formulated for an overseas market was imported into the UK.

HELD: This was a misrepresentation that the manufacturer considered that quality of product to be suitable for the UK.

Associated Newspapers can be put in this category. Where the other market is in the EEA, see also 'The free movement of goods' later in the chapter—an EU defence may apply.

Was the misrepresentation effective (did it confuse people)?

A trader may use another's sign, or even state a direct connection with another trader, but yet not be passing-off because the misrepresentation does not actually fool anyone. All the circumstances in which the defendant markets and sells its products, or delivers its services, must be taken into account in deciding whether people are actually misled. The scope of the claimant's reputation and the similarity of the signs used by the parties are often the major factors.

Taittinger and others v Allbev Limited and another [1994] 4 All ER 75 (CA)

FACTS: Less sophisticated purchasers might have believed that the Allbev product 'Elderflower Champagne' was the same drink as the well-known sparkling French wine.

HELD: Only a substantial proportion (not a majority) of typical consumers for the product in question need be confused, and this was established in this case.

See 'Extended passing-off'.

An important factor is always the attitude of the typical consumer to the representation.

Clark v Associated Newspapers [1998] RPC 261

FACTS: See Chapter 4 'Key cases'. Evening newspapers are typically not read carefully.

HELD: Even though a careful reading would give a true impression, there was a misrepresentation that Mr Clark was the author of the articles.

Consumer reaction can be hard to predict—*Reckitt* is a case where consumer research evidence showed that there was confusion when it might not have been inferred from a consideration of the facts.

Another important factor is the area of trade involved. If the defendant and claimant operate in the same area there is a high likelihood of confusion. But the further apart from each other the areas of trade, the less likely it is that customers will think the two businesses are associated, even if they use identical brand names or signs. Where the business areas differ, the type of confusion is likely to be confusion as to some kind of trade association, rather than as to the actual source of the products or services.

In *Harrods v Harrodian School* [1996], the judge found that people dealing with the school would not think there was any trade association with the Harrods department store because of the very different areas of operation. Contrast this with *Lego*:

Lego v Lemelstrich [1983] FSR 155

FACTS: D made garden hose fittings under the same name as the well-known Danish toy company.

HELD: There was confusion despite the different product categories.

The misrepresentation was, or would have been, that of a trade association with the claimant, rather than a direct trade source in both *Harrods* and *Lego*.

In the case of local businesses (particularly service industries such as restaurants), the public will not necessarily think that businesses of the same name in different locations are related, especially if the name is commonplace (such as 'The King's Head' for a pub).

Proving confusion—evidence and inference

Customer confusion is not easy to prove. In many cases where an early injunction is obtained, evidence from the market will be impossible, as the defendant's product will not be available. Applications for early injunctions are very common in passing-off cases and many of the cases referred to arise from applications for early injunctions, not full trials. The court can *infer* a likelihood of confusion from all the circumstances.

Evidence from individual consumers can be used but is very expensive to obtain. In *Reckitt*, such evidence was crucial as the court would not otherwise have inferred confusion—similarly, in a case where confusion appears a likely inference, consumer evidence can counteract that. The courts are wary of accepting the results of surveys.

Where the competing products remain on the market, some evidence of how customers react to them will generally be required (eg complaints addressed to the wrong company, confused references in reviews, and so on).

Loss must be caused (damage to goodwill)

The most obvious type of loss that will be caused if an effective misrepresentation is proved will be lost sales for the claimant, as some potential customers will buy goods or services from the defendant by mistake. This is unlikely where the defendant's products do not compete directly with the claimant's. But other types of loss are recognized—the claimant does not have to actually quantify any loss provided there is some damage to goodwill.

- *Loss of actual or potential licensing or endorsement revenues*—see 'Character and personality merchandizing' for examples. The loss of this ability was also found in *Lego*.

- *No quality control*—if customers associate the claimant and defendant and there is a problem with the defendant's product, the claimant's reputation will suffer. This type of loss was also referred to in *Lego* and was the type of loss in *Associated Newspapers* (no control over the suitability of the content).

Annabel's (Berkeley Square) Ltd v G Schock [1972] FSR 261 (CA)

FACTS: An exclusive night club (claimant) was associated with an escort agency.

HELD: This would damage the reputation of the night club.

- *Damage by 'dilution' of the brand*—in *Harrods*, the High Court observed (*obiter*) that this type of damage might be sufficient to found an action in passing-off.

Particular cases

These cases involve scenarios that are best considered separately, though all the elements of passing-off must be present in them.

Character and personality merchandizing

A number of older cases had held that where a business was set up with reference to a well-known character or personality, the character had no passing-off rights (though copyright or defamation claims might arise). This situation has now changed. Whether this represents a change in the law or a change in how the law regards consumer understanding of licensing activities is unclear.

Mirage Studios and others v Counter-Feat Clothing Company Ltd and another [1991] FSR 145

FACTS: The owners of the rights in the cartoon series *Teenage Mutant Ninja Turtles* claimed that an unlicensed manufacturer of replica toys was passing-off.

HELD: The public were aware of copyright licensing and would think that the products were 'official'. Damage to goodwill would arise from the reduction in merchandizing opportunities.

In *Edmund Irvine, Tidswell Ltd v Talksport Ltd* [2002], this principle was extended to the business in product endorsement carried on by a racing driver, so that he could stop unauthorized use of his name. *Irvine* does not give a general right to celebrities, only to those who have developed an endorsement business which can be damaged.

'Reverse passing-off'

So far, there is only one case in this category, but it reinforces the origins of the tort in deceit:

Bristol Conservatories v Conservatories Custom Built [1989] RPC 455

FACTS: The defendant's salesman showed photographs of completed conservatories to potential customers as examples of the defendant's work. The photographs were in fact of the claimant's work.

HELD: This was a misrepresentation that damaged the claimant's goodwill and was passing-off.

This case remains controversial.

Extended passing-off

Although extended passing-off shares many aspects of ordinary passing-off, it contains one distinctive feature. In these cases, the courts recognize the protectability of a joint goodwill in relation to products with common features. The precise elements of this branch of the tort are set out in a series of cases involving food products, although it could apply in other areas. The basic elements were set out in:

Bollinger v Costa Brava Wine Co [1960] Ch 262

HELD:

- there must be a group of traders,
- who all sell a particular product that has certain defining properties,
- under a single name, which the public associates with products having those qualities.

Where this situation arises, even though each manufacturer will add its own brand name to the products, each of them can sue any other trader in passing-off where that trader is selling products under the common name that do not have the defining properties.

This cause of action has been used by French champagne manufacturers to prevent other drinks being called 'champagne' (as in *Bollinger* and *Taittinger* discussed earlier) and similarly for Scotch whisky, Parma ham, and vodka.

The scope of the cause of action is unclear in relation to how specific the defining properties need to be, and how closely a trader has to follow them to join the club—in *Chocosuisse v Cadbury Ltd* [1999], Swiss chocolate manufacturers did not all make chocolate to the same standards, but still succeeded.

Defence

If a defendant can show that they have a goodwill that is associated in the minds of their customers with a sign or name, then they will not be passing-off by using that name, even if the claimant can make out all the elements of the cause of action by reason of its goodwill. This is known as 'concurrent goodwill'.

Registered trade marks

Section and Article references in this chapter are to the Trade Marks Act 1994 of the current version of the Trade Marks Directive, 2008/95/EC.

General concepts
The powers of a trade mark

Like other registered rights, trade marks have two distinct powers:

- the power to block registrations of later marks (defensive);
- the power to prevent use by others of the mark (offensive).

In many respects, similar rules apply to both the defensive and offensive powers.

Key concept—the consumer for the type of goods or services in question

Just as patents have the skilled person and registered designs have the informed user, in trade marks law the important person is the consumer. Questions such as the **distinctiveness** of a mark, or whether two marks are so similar as to cause confusion, are assessed with reference to the consumer.

Trade mark applications

A trade mark registration contains (in addition to administrative details such as the name of the proprietor and so on) two vital pieces of information:

- the mark itself;
- a description of the goods covered by the registration.

The absolute rights given by the registration only cover that mark when used in relation to those goods (though rights extend outside this core if certain facts are demonstrated). A trade mark applicant must either use or intend to use the mark in relation to the goods. It is not possible to dream up a good brand name, register it, and thereby acquire rights.

The law on registrability is framed in terms of various grounds of objection that can be raised to trade mark applications. These are summarized in Figure 9.1 and discussed under the following headings.

Applications are examined against the absolute grounds of objection but not the relative ones—it is up to holders of prior rights to object to applications, or challenge registered marks, on those grounds.

Figure 9.1 Registrability of signs as trade marks—a quick guide

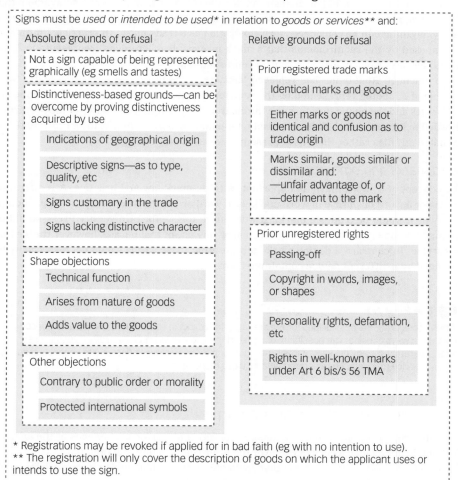

Signs must be *used* or *intended to be used** in relation to *goods or services*** and:

Absolute grounds of refusal

Not a sign capable of being represented graphically (eg smells and tastes)

Distinctiveness-based grounds—can be overcome by proving distinctiveness acquired by use

    Indications of geographical origin

    Descriptive signs—as to type, quality, etc

    Signs customary in the trade

    Signs lacking distinctive character

Shape objections

    Technical function

    Arises from nature of goods

    Adds value to the goods

Other objections

    Contrary to public order or morality

    Protected international symbols

Relative grounds of refusal

Prior registered trade marks

    Identical marks and goods

    Either marks or goods not identical and confusion as to trade origin

    Marks similar, goods similar or dissimilar and:
    —unfair advantage of, or
    —detriment to the mark

Prior unregistered rights

    Passing-off

    Copyright in words, images, or shapes

    Personality rights, defamation, etc

    Rights in well-known marks under Art 6 bis/s 56 TMA

* Registrations may be revoked if applied for in bad faith (eg with no intention to use).
** The registration will only cover the description of goods on which the applicant uses or intends to use the sign.

The basic definition of a trade mark—'a sign capable of graphical representation'

Section 1 (Art 2) gives the basic definition of a trade mark as follows:

(1) In this Act a 'trade mark' means any sign capable of being represented graphically which is capable of distinguishing goods or services of one undertaking from those of other undertakings.

A trade mark may, in particular, consist of words (including personal names), designs, letters, numerals or the shape of goods or their packaging.

The TMA 1994 was a major change—under the TMA 1938 only signs and symbols that could be 'applied to' goods were allowed. The list given in s 1(1) is not exhaustive, so in theory anything can be considered for registration as a trade mark. In practice, limitations are imposed by the requirements that a mark is 'capable of graphical representation' and distinctive (see 'Not capable of graphical representation').

The amended Regulation has replaced 'capable of being represented graphically' with 'capable of . . . being represented on the register in a manner which enables the competent authorities and the public to determine the clear and precise subject matter of the protection afforded to its proprietor'. This will enable, for example, moving marks to be represented as animated .gif files rather than, as at present, a series of static images.

Word marks and other marks

The concept of a 'word mark' is important in trade mark law and practice. A registration can cover a word or phrase (a word mark) or a word or phrase when written in a particular way (which would be a device mark). A word mark for 'Oxford University Press' would be infringed by, and could block the registration of, any use of that phrase, however the writing was styled. In contrast, a device mark incorporating those words would not necessarily be infringed by a different device containing them.

✔ 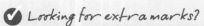 *Looking for extra marks?*

When considering the possibilities for registering trade marks in relation to a particular proposed venture, always consider the possibility of registering word marks for any words or slogans used and, separately, for any devices or logos incorporating them, packaging design and shape, and so on. Often a device mark can be registered when a word mark cannot.

Absolute grounds of objection

Absolute grounds of objection take into consideration all the circumstances of the application, but do not include a consideration of the prior rights of any individual.

Section 3(1)(a) (Art 3(1)(a)) states that applications can be objected to if they are for 'signs which do not satisfy the requirements of section 1(1)'—that is the requirements for a sign, capable of distinguishing and capable of graphical representation.

> **Philips v Remington [2003] RPC 2 (ECJ)**
>
> **HELD:** It is not necessary to consider the meaning of 'capable of distinguishing' as in practice the issue of the actual distinctive character of a mark will be considered under **s 3(1)(b)/Art 3(1)(b)** (marks lacking distinctive character: see 'Devoid of distinctive character **(s 3(1)(b))**').

Not a sign

The need for a sign prevents very general concepts being registered:

> **Dyson Ltd v Registrar of Trade Marks (C-321/03) [2007] Bus LR 787S**
>
> **FACTS:** An application for a transparent dust bin on a vacuum cleaner.
>
> **HELD:** This was a property of the product, not a 'sign' within the meaning of the Directive.

Not capable of graphical representation

This is the main factor that causes problems under this section.

The application form for a trade mark contains a 10cm x 10cm box within which the representation of the mark must be put. Where the mark applied for is a word mark (see 'Word marks and other marks') the word is simply typed in capitals in the box. For device marks, a copy of the device is put there. For shape marks, a relief drawing or photograph of the article is used. In the case of shape marks, some applicants register a series of marks each with a different view of the product. Colours, sounds, smells, and tastes clearly present particular problems when it comes to completing the form.

The leading case in relation to graphical representation is *Ralf Sieckmann v Deutsches Patent- und Markenamt* [2003]. Here the ECJ held that a trade mark:

> may consist of a sign which is not in itself capable of being perceived visually, provided that it can be represented graphically, particularly by means of images, lines or characters, and that the representation is clear, precise, self-contained, easily accessible, intelligible, durable and objective.

Colour and combination of colour marks

Here we are talking about marks where the applicant is seeking to assert exclusive rights over the use of a colour or colour combination, however it may be used. The following considerations do not apply to device marks that make use of colour, or marks consisting of a shape in a particular colour.

> **Libertel Groep BV v Benelux-Merkenbureau (C-104/01) [2004] FSR 4**
>
> **FACTS:** An application for the colour orange by the telecommunications company.
>
> **HELD:** A recognized colour-matching system such as Pantone® may be used to define colours, but in some cases a combination of a sample of the colour and a verbal description could be sufficient.

Registered trade marks

✳✳✳✳✳✳✳✳✳✳

Single-colour marks are rare because of the difficulty of establishing distinctiveness in a single colour—see 'The distinctiveness-based objections'.

As for combinations of colours:

> **Heidelberger Bauchemie GmbH (C-49/02) [2004] ETMR 99 (ECJ)**
>
> **FACTS:** The application specified two colours without stating how they were arranged.
>
> **HELD:** This was not acceptable; a colour combination could be registered if 'the application for registration includes a systematic arrangement associating the colours concerned in a predetermined and uniform way'.

Sounds

> **Shield Mark BV v Kist (C-283/01) [2004] RPC 17 (ECJ)**
>
> **FACTS:** A mark consisting of the sound of a cock crow was described by a verbal description and an onomatopoeic reference ('Kukelekuuuuu', as is used in Belgium).
>
> HELD: This did not meet the **Sieckmann** test. A tune written in musical notation was acceptable, but a sequence of notes without any indication of their duration, or reference to the name of the tune, was not.

Smells and flavours—known as 'olfactory marks'

In its early days OHIM allowed an application for 'the smell of new-mown grass' in respect of 'tennis balls'. Since that case, the EUIPO has changed its practice and this was endorsed by the ECJ in *Sieckmann*. There is no way adequately to represent a smell or taste, so they cannot be registered (the tennis balls registration has been allowed to lapse).

✅ Looking for extra marks?

It should not be assumed that the amended Regulation wording noted above will alter this situation, as it will remain difficult to overcome the fundamental issue of identification even with non-graphical forms of representation. See Onur Sahin, 'The Past, the Present and the Future of Colour and Smell Marks' (2016) 38(8) EIPR 504.

The distinctiveness-based objections

Section 3 (Art 1) is as follows:

(1) The following shall not be registered—

. . .

(b) trade marks which are devoid of any distinctive character,

(c) trade marks which consist exclusively of signs or indications which may serve, in trade, to designate the kind, quality, quantity, intended purpose, value, geographical origin, the time of production of goods or of rendering of services, or other characteristics of goods or services,

(d) trade marks which consist exclusively of signs or indications which have become custom-ary in the current language or in the bona fide and established practices of the trade:

Provided that, a trade mark shall not be refused registration by virtue of paragraph (b), (c) or (d) above if, before the date of application for registration, it has in fact acquired a distinctive character as a result of the use made of it.

Marks falling within (c) and (d) are *assumed* not to be distinctive (because of their descrip-tive nature), but they can nevertheless be registered if distinctiveness is proved. Marks that do not fall within (c) or (d) will only be objected to under (b) if there is a reason to doubt their distinctive character. In practice, this means that invented words and logos are unlikely to be objected to, but that unusual marks such as shapes and sounds often are, and distinctive-ness has to be demonstrated.

Devoid of distinctive character (s 3(1)(b))

Distinctive character is judged through the eyes of the consumer. Consumers tend to look separately for a brand identifier and a product description, and to be guided by the practice in that product area. The way products of a particular type are generally presented is relevant.

BORCO-Marken-Import Matthiesen GmbH & Co KG v OHIM (C-265/09 P) [2011] ETMR 4

FACTS: The single letter 'α' for beer was applied for.

HELD: Distinctive character is a 'global consideration' in each case; that is, all the circumstances of the mark applied for and the market for the goods concerned must be considered—this mark failed the test.

Shape-of-product marks are often objected to on this ground. The ECJ has held in a number of cases that the shape of a product, even if it is unique to a particular brand, is not distinctive:

Mag Instrument Inc v OHIM (C-136/02 P) [2005] ETMR 46

HELD: The shape of LED torches made by a market leader was not distinctive of the products of that manufacturer because customers would not think of it as a brand identifier.

A 'shape-of-product' mark has also been refused for the shape of a fork-lift truck. An impor-tant point arises from this case—de facto exclusivity (perhaps arising from being the first to market, or design rights) does not necessarily imply distinctiveness.

Applications for single-colour marks will face stiff opposition on this ground, and this is why very few single-colour applications have been registered. Here are a few—note that

Registered trade marks
✳✳✳✳✳✳✳✳✳✳✳

they are all household-name brands. Heinz have registered their turquoise colour for 'beans'; Kraft Foods have registered lilac for chocolate in connection with their 'Milka' brand; and Orange Telecommunications have registered orange for certain telecommunications products and services.

Marks consisting of single letters or short initializations are generally viewed as lacking distinctive character, as in *BORCO*.

Descriptive marks (s 3(1)(c))

The ECJ has developed the 'free to use' doctrine here. Where a mark might legitimately be used by a trader in the goods or services in question to describe them, then they should be free to do so, meaning that this objection should be raised in relation to applications for that mark.

> ### *Koninklijke KPN Nederland NV v Benelux-Merkenbureau* (C-363/99)[2004] ETMR 57
>
> **FACTS:** The mark applied for was 'Postkantor'; the Dutch for 'post office' is 'post kantor'.
>
> **HELD:** Where a mark consisted entirely of descriptive words, it was descriptive regardless of whether the words were put together in an unusual way. It was not relevant that the mark as a whole was not the most usual way such products might be described if they could be described that way.

Customary marks (s 3(1)(d))

It is difficult to distinguish customary from descriptive marks. In cases where a word is used in a customary way in the trade, and yet is not descriptive as far as consumers are concerned, this objection will be relevant (and it can be raised even if a descriptive objection could also be made).

Distinctiveness acquired by use (s 3(1) proviso)

Windsurfing Chiemsee [1999] illustrates how the 'free to use' doctrine relates to distinctiveness acquired by use. The ECJ firmly rejected arguments that the 'free to use' doctrine should prevail over acquired distinctiveness—if distinctiveness can be shown, then the mark is no longer free to use.

Thus, where a mark is applied for on the basis of intended rather than actual use, if a distinctiveness objection is raised, then the application must fail and the applicant must wait until distinctiveness has developed through use, and then apply again.

The shape objections (s 3(2)/Art 3.1(e))

Shape objections are set out in s 3(2):

(2) A sign shall not be registered as a trade mark if it consists exclusively of—

    (a) the shape which results from the nature of the goods themselves,

    (b) the shape of goods which is necessary to obtain a technical result, or

    (c) the shape which gives substantial value to the goods.

The Regulation has amended these grounds so they apply to the shape 'or other characteristics' of the goods. This recognizes that the underlying basis for these objections, that functional marks should not be registered, is valid for all types of mark.

The 'nature of the goods' exclusion would, for example, prevent a mark in the shape of a tennis racket being registered for tennis rackets.

The 'technical function' objection is different from the concept of 'dictated solely by function' seen with registered designs: be careful not to get the two mixed up. This is explained in the *Lego Juris* case.

Lego Juris A/S v OHIM (C-48/09 P) [2010] ETMR 63

FACTS: The Danish toy manufacturer applied for registration of the shape of its toy bricks, which included features for interconnecting them.

HELD: For a shape to fall within this ground of objection:

- all the essential elements of the mark must fulfil a technical function (the presence of non-essential non-technical elements did not matter);
- it did not matter that the technical function could be achieved by a different shape;
- the essential elements of a mark are its most important elements—and this must be decided on a case-by-case basis (the Court was unwilling to prescribe detailed rules for this).

  The Lego bricks fell within the ground, and the shape objections could not be overcome by acquired distinctiveness.

Lego confirmed and developed the doctrine from *Philips* (discussed in 'Absolute grounds of objection'). The Court was mindful that trade mark rights *may* last forever, and that as a matter of policy they should not be used to extend patent protection.

The 'substantial value' ground is less often raised. Shapes with a strong aesthetic element are likely to be excluded on this ground.

Bang & Olufsen A/S v OHIM (GC) (T-508/08) [2012] ETMR 10

FACTS: B&O sought to register the shape of a loudspeaker, which was designed to be visually attractive, like a sculpture, and was 'an important selling point'.

HELD: The mark should be refused on this ground and similar public policy considerations applied as for the other 'shape' objections.

Revision tip

Many of the 'shape' cases also involve distinctiveness issues. Make sure you separate the issues—whenever considering the registrability of an unusual mark, such as the shape of goods, consider distinctiveness. Most unusual mark applications fail on this ground.

Other objections

By s 3(3), marks cannot be registered if they are deceptive or contrary to public policy or accepted principles of morality.

Deceptiveness covers descriptive marks where the description is inaccurate. For example, the word 'APPLE' cannot be registered for pears or other fruit. It would, of course, face a descriptive objection if restricted to apples, but is registered for computer equipment (as computers have nothing to do with fruit).

The EUIPO has refused some marks on the morality ground, including 'JESUS' for clothing (on the basis that it would offend religious sensibilities). Obscene phrases have also been refused.

Marks may be refused if their use is prohibited by law (eg laws concerning product labelling); some emblems are specially protected (national flags, images of the Royal family, etc) by s 4.

By s 3(5), trade marks can be objected to if the application was made in bad faith—this is dealt with later in relation to opposing trade marks.

Relative grounds of objection

Blocking powers of prior registered marks

The Directive, Act, and Regulation all define the blocking power of a trade mark and the rights it gives its owner to prevent use of the mark in essentially identical terms. These powers can be represented as spheres of widening power, as shown in Figure 9.2:

The ECJ has consistently interpreted this to mean that identical doctrines should be followed in relation to the powers of a registered trade mark in these three spheres.

For this reason, some cases discussed under the following three headings are infringement cases rather than opposition cases.

Figure 9.2 The powers of a trade mark

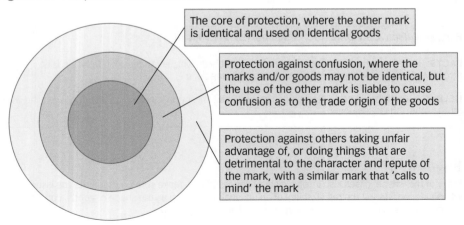

The core of protection, where the other mark is identical and used on identical goods

Protection against confusion, where the marks and/or goods may not be identical, but the use of the other mark is liable to cause confusion as to the trade origin of the goods

Protection against others taking unfair advantage of, or doing things that are detrimental to the character and repute of the mark, with a similar mark that 'calls to mind' the mark

For the purposes of blocking, an earlier mark includes an earlier national trade mark registration or Community trade mark.

Absolute power (same mark, same goods)

It would be inconsistent with the core concepts of a trade mark if one mark could be registered by two different proprietors for the same goods. So s 5(1) states:

(1) A trade mark shall not be registered if it is identical with an earlier trade mark and the goods or services for which the trade mark is applied for are identical with the goods or services for which the earlier trade mark is protected.

Two marks are considered 'identical' if the differences are so insignificant that they will go unnoticed by the average consumer (*SA Societe LTJ Diffusion v Sadas Vertbaudet SA* [2003]). Thus, in the case of a mark that is a common word, a misspelling of it would probably be regarded as identical.

Registrations are for identical goods if they both cover the same goods—even if one or both marks also cover goods not covered by the other. (In such a case, it may be possible to register the mark for those goods not covered by the earlier mark—subject to the confusion test in the following section.)

Further blocking power where there is confusion (mark and/or goods not the same)

In addition, the Directive states in **Art 4(1)**:

(b) if because of its identity with, or similarity to, the earlier trade mark and the identity or similarity of the goods or services covered by the trade marks, there exists a likelihood of confusion on the part of the public, the likelihood of confusion includes the likelihood of association with the earlier trade mark.

The ECJ first stated what the confusion test was in *Sabel v Puma* [1998]:

- the confusion must be confusion as to the trade origin of the goods, either that the goods come from the same undertaking or that they come from economically linked undertakings;

- the test is a single global test in which all factors must be taken into account (including those set out in the (now **11th**) **recital** to the Directive, which are 'in particular . . . the recognition of the trade mark on the market, the association which can be made with the used or registered sign, the degree of similarity between the trade mark and the sign and between the goods or services identified'). The factors to be taken into account include:

  - the visual, aural, or conceptual similarity of the marks bearing in mind, in particular, their distinctive and dominant components;

  - the distinctiveness of the earlier mark—the more distinctive the earlier mark, the more the likelihood of confusion;

Registered trade marks

✳✳✳✳✳✳✳✳✳✳✳

- the earlier mark can be distinctive per se or because of the reputation it enjoys with the public; but
- the mere fact that the public might associate the marks with each other as a result of their analogous semantic content is not in itself a ground for concluding that there is a likelihood of confusion.

More recent ECJ cases have explained further aspects of the doctrine:

Lloyd Schuhfabrik Meyer & Co GmbH v Klijsen Handel BV (C-342/97) [1999] ETMR 690

HELD: The average consumer is 'deemed to be reasonably well-informed and reasonably observant and circumspect . . . must place his trust in the imperfect picture of [the marks] that he has kept in his mind . . . [his] level of attention is likely to vary according to the category of goods or services in question'.

This person is thus somewhat more careful than the customer in passing-off.

Marca Mode CV v Adidas AG and Adidas Benelux BV (C-102/07) [2008] ETMR 44

FACTS: D used a two-stripe motif on sportswear similar to Adidas' well-known three-stripe motif.

HELD: However well-known a mark, there must still be a likelihood of confusion as to origin—a 'risk of association' was not sufficient.

Unfortunately, the wording of TMA, s 5(2) (and the equivalent infringement section, s 10(2)) do not follow the exact wording of the Directive, and can be interpreted as requiring a two-stage test. First, are the goods 'similar'? Secondly, if they are, is there a likelihood of confusion? This is clearly incorrect in view of the decisions of the ECJ that it is a 'global consideration'. Whether or not things are similar is not relevant; the test is confusion arising from similarity (which can range from 'only slightly similar' to 'almost identical').

Revision tip

Note the preceding paragraph carefully—some older cases and materials that are still referred to talk of a two-stage test, particularly in relation to 'similar goods'. This is a good example of how a simple reading of a statute can lead to an erroneous impression of the law.

Extra blocking powers of marks with a reputation

Article 4(4) of the Directive states that:

4. Any Member State may, in addition, provide that a trade mark shall not be registered or, if registered, shall be liable to be declared invalid where, and to the extent that:

   (a) the trade mark is identical with, or similar to, an earlier national trade mark within the meaning of paragraph 2 and is to be, or has been, registered for goods or services which are not similar to those for which the earlier trade mark is registered, where the earlier trade mark has a reputation in the Member State concerned and where the use of the later trade mark without due cause would take unfair advantage of, or be detrimental to, the distinctive character or the repute of the earlier trade mark.

Davidoff & Cie SA v Gofkid Ltd (C-292/00) [2003] ETMR 42

HELD: Where **Art 4(4)** refers to the goods or services being 'not similar', that should be read as 'either similar or not similar' in order to avoid nonsensical situations arising. Most states have implemented provisions in these terms, including the UK in **s 5(3)**—which does not refer to use in relation to 'not similar' goods or services.

A provision in those terms is in the Regulation, and the amended Regulation reflects the *Davidoff* interpretation.

Section 5(3) in fact involves two blocking powers, one involving unfair advantage and one detriment—and the case-law deals with these separately. However, all pose the questions of what 'reputation' and 'similar' mean.

General Motors Corp v Yplon SA (C-375/97) [2000] RPC 572

HELD: A reputation is not the same thing as goodwill; it simply means being known to the public. The relevant public are the consumers for the type of goods on which the mark sought to be blocked is used.

Adidas-Salomon AG v Fitnessworld Trading Ltd (C-408/01) [2004] ETMR 10

HELD: Confusion is not required for similarity; what is necessary is a 'connection or link', made by the relevant public, between the two marks.

In *Intel Corporation Inc v CPM United Kingdom Ltd* [2009], the ECJ said that the use of one mark must 'bring to mind' the other. The Court also held that all that has to be shown is a risk, that is not hypothetical, of unfair advantage or detriment.

The nature of unfair advantage and detriment has been extensively dealt with in recent cases.

Unfair advantage without due cause

In *L'Oreal SA v Bellure NV* [2009], the ECJ held that any use that took advantage and was without due cause was unfair, and further held that use of a similar mark on packaging in a 'look-alike' product did not have a due cause. The Court of Appeal was not happy with this judgment when the case returned to it, but could do little about it.

As for advantage, in *L'Oreal* the High Court had found as a fact that Bellure could sell products in the 'look-alike' packaging at a higher profit margin than plainly packaged products, which was a clear advantage.

Detriment to the distinctive character or repute without due cause

L'Oreal does not place many barriers in the way of enforcing a trade mark under the unfair advantage heading. The ECJ has not been so lenient when considering detriment. In *Intel*, the ECJ held that detriment means that the 'economic behaviour' of consumers of the owner's products is affected—that means that they must be prepared to pay less for products, or buy fewer of them. It will be difficult to prove a risk of this in many cases where the use of the mark by the other party is not clearly going to undermine the brand, though it may be considered a bit cheeky.

Blocking powers of holders of other rights

The Directive recognizes that earlier legal rights can block a trade mark registration. The Act in s 5(4) states that any earlier legal right that could prevent the use in the UK of the trade mark will block its registration. The Act mentions in particular copyright and passing-off, but design rights could also block a registration, as could the law of defamation or privacy (eg in the case of slogans or photographs).

The law of passing-off is obviously very important as it gives blocking power to earlier marks that are not registered. Rights of well-known marks under TMA, s 56 can also block registration—see 'Statutory right for well-known marks'.

Rights of trade mark owners and defences

The Directive, Regulation, and Act talk in terms of the rights conferred by a trade mark. Under Art 5(1) and (2) (s 10(1)–(3)), the trade mark proprietor is given powers to stop third parties from using the mark or a similar one that are phrased in identical language to the three blocking powers described above. The doctrine and relevant cases (some of which are in fact infringement cases) were described earlier, but the questions will be asked in different contexts, as to which some legal issues arise.

Section 10 talks of the potential infringer using a 'sign', to distinguish it from the 'mark' that is registered. It also (for all three powers) requires that the sign is used in the course of trade in relation to goods or services. The ECJ uses the doctrine of the 'functions of a trade mark' to both define and limit the scope of trade mark infringement.

Celine Sarl v Celine SA (C-17/06) [2007] ETMR 80 (ECJ)

FACTS: The mark/sign was identical, but D's use was in its company name and on a shop front selling clothes, whereas C's mark was registered for clothes.

HELD: There are four conditions for same mark/same goods infringement:

- that use must be in the course of trade;
- it must be without the consent of the proprietor of the mark;
- it must be in respect of goods or services which are identical to those for which the mark is registered; and
- it must affect or be liable to affect the functions of the trade mark, in particular its essential function of guaranteeing to consumers the origin of the goods or services.

The court developed the concept in *Interflora*:

Interflora Inc v Marks & Spencer Plc (C-323/09) [2012] ETMR 1

The functions of a trade mark are: identifying the goods as those of the proprietor (the essential function); guarantee of quality; communication; investment; and advertising.

A trade mark proprietor should be able to protect all these functions by exercising its rights under EU trade marks law.

Thus the functions serve to interpret the powers given to marks in the Act, but also to limit them—activity that does not affect the functions of a mark will not infringe it.

Same mark/same goods situations—(s 10(1)/Art 5(1)(a))

Not all uses of the same mark in connection with the same goods will infringe a trade mark. *Celine* held that use of a mark on a shop front did not amount to use in relation to the products sold in the shop unless the use established a link between the sign and the goods, and the essential function will only be affected if 'consumers are liable to interpret it as designating the origin of the goods . . .'. Use to describe genuine products for sale has been held not to infringe. Referring to branded products in a book will not infringe. What of actually fixing the mark to the goods?

Arsenal Football Club Plc v Reed (C-206/01) [2003] RPC 9

FACTS: Mr Reed sold scarves and other clothing bearing badges of the club that were registered as trade marks in respect of clothing.

HELD: Placing an identical sign on identical goods was use in relation to those goods and affected the essential function. The High Court had found that customers did not think Mr Reed's produce was official. The ECJ did not think this was relevant and noted that post-sale misunderstanding might occur.

Arsenal had failed in an action for passing-off as there was no confusion at the point of sale—this illustrates the increased protection a trade mark registration gives.

A contrasting case is *Opel*:

Adam Opel AG v Autec (C-48/05) [2004] ETMR 2

FACTS: The Opel logo was registered for real cars and toys and D used it on scale model toy cars (so same mark and same goods).

HELD: If the public would not perceive that the toys came from Opel or an economically linked organization, there was no effect on the essential function, though there was use in relation to toys. The German court subsequently held that there was no infringement because the German public expected accurate scale models to include logos, so would not perceive a link.

Registered trade marks

✱✱✱✱✱✱✱✱✱✱

In *L'Oreal*, the defendant used comparison charts to match its 'smell-alike' products to the claimants, by brand name. In deciding the case, the ECJ gave a strong indication that as the use by the defendant went beyond the 'purely descriptive' the advertising function had been affected, although the essential function had not. The Court of Appeal reluctantly applied this test and found infringement under s 10(1) while criticizing the vagueness and difficulty associated with the non-essential functions. It questioned why such subtlety was needed given the defence afforded by s 11(2)/Art 6(1) (discussed under 'Limitations on the rights of trade mark owners (defences)').

The law in this area has developed via cases involving internet marketing and selling operations:

Google France Sarl and another v Louis Vuitton Malletier SA (C-236/08) [2010] RPC 19

FACTS: Google's practice of selling 'Adwords' involves a link to the Adword buyer's advertisement appearing prominently and separately when the Adword is searched for. Traders sometimes purchase rivals' registered word marks as Adwords.

HELD: Google itself was not infringing the essential function of the trade mark by selling Adwords as *its* use did not lead to misdirection. But the buyers would infringe if their linked advertisement did not enable a normally informed and reasonably attentive internet user to determine whether there was an economic link between the proprietor of the mark and the advertiser.

The other powers of a trade mark

Although the doctrine of the functions of a trade mark will apply in these cases, the requirements for confusion, unfair advantage, or detriment define infringement—the ECJ noted this in *Google France*.

Infringing acts

TMA, s 10(4) states that:

(4) For the purposes of this section a person uses a sign if, in particular, he—

    (a) affixes it to goods or the packaging thereof;

    (b) offers or exposes goods for sale, puts them on the market or stocks them for those purposes under the sign, or offers or supplies services under the sign;

    (c) imports or exports goods under the sign; or

    (d) uses the sign on business papers or in advertising.

This must be understood to be subject to the requirement for there to be use in relation to goods and interference with the functions of a trade mark (see above, particularly *Opel*). The Directive says these things 'inter alia *may* be prohibited'.

The amended Regulation includes two further things which may amount to infringement in the equivalent of Article 5(1): use of a mark as a company name and use of a mark in an advertisement that does not comply with the Directive (see 'Limitations on the rights of trade mark owners (defences)' below). These may not add anything to the case-law (*O2* below and *Celine*).

Of more practical significance is **s 10(5)**, which states:

(5) A person who applies a registered trade mark to material intended to be used for labelling or packaging goods, as a business paper, or for advertising goods or services, shall be treated as a party to any use of the material which infringes the registered trade mark if when he applied the mark he knew or had reason to believe that the application of the mark was not duly authorised by the proprietor or a licensee.

This is clearly intended as a modification or clarification of the law of **joint tortfeasorship** in relation to trade mark infringement, rather than an act of infringement itself. That is important—in *Google* and other internet infringement cases the ECJ held that whether Google and others were liable for trade mark infringement as joint tortfeasors was a matter for the law of the Member States, as the law of joint liability has not been harmonized by the EU.

Limitations on the rights of trade mark owners (defences)

Section 11(2) (Art 6(1)) is as follows:

(2) A registered trade mark is not infringed by—

(a) the use by a person of his own name or address,

(b) the use of indications concerning the kind, quality, quantity, intended purpose, value, geographical origin, the time of production of goods or of rendering of services, or other characteristics of goods or services, or

(c) the use of the trade mark where it is necessary to indicate the intended purpose of a product or service (in particular, as accessories or spare parts),

provided the use is in accordance with honest practices in industrial or commercial matters.

Indications of kind, etc covers a wide range of activities in which legitimate use of another's mark is clearly warranted (eg 'runs on Windows 10').

Bayerische Motoren Werke AG v Deenik (C-63/97) [1999] ETMR 339

FACTS: Mr Deenik said that he repaired BMWs and was a 'specialist in BMWs' (which was true), though he was not an official dealer.

HELD: His use was in relation to his services because they were so closely connected with BMW's products, but he had the benefit of the defence as he was not indicating a trade association with the German car company, and was complying with honest practices.

Note that this was before the Court developed its doctrine of the functions of a mark.

In *Celine* (see 'Rights of trade mark owners and defences') honest practices involved a 'duty to act fairly in relation to the legitimate interests of the trade mark proprietor'. It was for the national court to decide, but the extent of the link indicated was relevant.

A more difficult area is comparative advertising, where one trader refers to another's mark in order to sell his goods, by making a comparison.

Registered trade marks

✷✷✷✷✷✷✷✷✷✷✷✷

O2 Holdings Ltd v Hutchison 3G Ltd (C-533/06) [2008] RPC 33 (ECJ)

FACTS: H used a picture of bubbles similar to O's bubbles logo, thereby intending to refer to O and make a product comparison (a similar mark/identical goods case).

HELD: If there was no confusion there was no infringement (the fact that it was a comparative advertisement did not alter this). If there was infringement, in order to comply with the honest practices requirement, the comparative advertisement had to fall within the **Comparative Advertising Directive (2006/114/EC)**. That Directive outlaws comparative advertisements that are not fair and balanced (a full analysis is beyond the scope of this book).

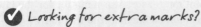 ✓ *Looking for extra marks?*

Section 11(2) provides an easy answer to many problems where use of a trade mark appears incidental or descriptive. But, in such cases, there may be no need to rely on it because there has been no infringing use at all (see 'Infringing acts'). Always consider 'use in relation to' and the functions of a trade mark alongside the applicability of any defence. The issues overlap (which was what the Court of Appeal complained of in *L'Oreal*).

The s 10(6) problem

TMA, s 10(6) reads as follows:

(6) Nothing in the preceding provisions of this section shall be construed as preventing the use of a registered trade mark by any person for the purpose of identifying goods or services as those of the proprietor or a licensee.

But any such use otherwise than in accordance with honest practices in industrial or commercial matters shall be treated as infringing the registered trade mark if the use without due cause takes unfair advantage of, or is detrimental to, the distinctive character or repute of the trade mark.

There are no equivalent provisions in the Directive and of course s 10(6) will not be interpreted in a way that is incompatible with it. The best approach is to ignore it and consider all cases in this area under s 11(2)/Art 6(1), which is the approach taken by the UK courts.

Maintaining and opposing trade marks

In addition to paying the renewal fees for a trade mark, the basic rule for proprietors is 'use it or lose it'. Under TMA, s 46(1), registrations can be revoked if the trade mark has not been used for a continuous period of five years, or within five years of the application being made. They can also be revoked if, *because of the use made of them*, they have become misleading. So marks must not only be used, they must be used carefully.

Trade marks can be assigned and licensed, but bearing in mind the point made earlier, any licence must include terms making sure that the mark is used properly. Most owners include quality control provisions in trade mark licences, as the value of a brand (which affects the ability to license in the future) is affected by the quality of goods sold under it.

Trade marks may also be 'declared invalid'. Roughly speaking, invalidity deals with issues arising when the mark was applied for; revocation to matters arising after. Marks may be declared invalid on the ground that any of the main requirements for registration noted earlier do not apply. There is one important proviso to this—if an objection is made on a distinctiveness-based ground (s 3(1)(b)–(d)), then distinctiveness acquired by use since the registration of the mark will defeat the opposition.

Any person may apply to have a trade mark revoked or declared invalid—as with patents and designs, oppositions to registrations frequently arise by way of counterclaims in litigation.

Statutory right for well-known marks

Under Art 6 bis of the Paris Convention, implemented by TMA, s 56, proprietors of marks that are well known in one jurisdiction have rights to block the registration of that mark, or obtain injunctive relief against the use of it, in other jurisdictions. This applies even where there is no trading presence or trade mark registration in the overseas jurisdiction. The right extends to 'imitations' of the mark, but there must be confusion.

Remedies

The usual remedies are available. Because of the effect on the claimant's goodwill, applications for interim injunctions are common in trade mark and passing-off cases.

While loss is an element of passing-off, a claimant does not have to be able to quantify any loss (see 'Loss must be caused (damage to goodwill)'). For trade mark infringement no loss need be proved. Where damages are sought, they will be quantified on the basis of either lost sales or a reasonable royalty basis, as with other rights.

In trade mark cases, orders for the delivery-up and destruction of goods bearing the mark are available.

The free movement of goods

See Chapter 1. There is a particular rule of EU law that can be relevant here. Where the quality of the goods has been changed, or where the value of an underlying IP right will be affected, the IP right can be enforced by way of exception to the rules on free movement.

This is important for brand owners. Repackaging of some products means the original trade mark cannot be used on them. Luxury brand owners can restrict sales of their product to those through their official stockists, even though their products become available on the 'grey market'.

Copad SA v Christian Dior Couture SA and others (C-59/08) [2009] ETMR 40

HELD: To avoid the free movement of goods defence, the brand owner will have to show that their brand value is based on an aura of exclusivity that will be damaged by the products being available through unofficial channels (such as the internet) at low prices.

Other related rights

The following legal rights are closely related to passing-off and trade marks, but are not dealt with in this book:

- trade libel, or the tort of malicious falsehood when applied to a trader's goods or services;
- the detailed law governing comparative advertising under **Directive 2006/114/EC**;
- the law implementing the **Unfair Commercial Practices Directive (2005/29/EC)**, which may in some situations provide protection that overlaps with passing-off;
- the law protecting designations of origin and regional specialities—these can be registered and protected according to EU law.

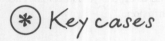 *Key cases*

Case	Facts	Principle
Reckitt & Colman Products Ltd v Borden Inc (No 3) [1990] RPC 341 (HL)	In *Reckitt*, the product was preserved lemon juice and the sign was the lemon-sized, lemon-coloured, and lemon-shaped plastic containers in which Reckitt sold juice under the name 'Jif'. The High Court found as a fact (based on evidence from buyers) that a substantial proportion of customers believed they were buying the Reckitt product when they purchased the Borden product.	The descriptive nature of the sign (the packaging) did not prevent a finding of passing-off where all the elements of the cause of action were made out, as here.
Anheuser-Busch Inc v Budejovicky Budvar NP [1984] FSR 413	The claimants' beer (a major US brand) was well known in the UK under the name 'Budweiser' but not on sale here. The defendants' beer (from former Czechoslovakia) was on sale under the same name (the name of a town in the Czech Republic).	The claimants had no goodwill in the UK because they had no customers here, in the sense that their product was not on sale in the UK.
Starbucks (HK) Ltd v British Sky Broadcasting Group Plc [2015] UKSC 31	The claimant sued (inter alia) in passing-off based on a television service available via a website under the name NOW TV. This service could be accessed in the UK via the internet, but not subscribed to as a paid-for service.	The UK viewers of the service were not customers and so there was no goodwill. For goodwill to arise, people in the UK would have had to be able to subscribe to or order a subscription from the UK. If this seemed harsh, s 56 TMA needed to be borne in mind.

Case	Facts	Principle
Harrods v Harrodian School [1996] RPC 697 (CA)	C was a well-known department store; D's school was on the site of the store's former sports ground. C sued in passing-off. Although the public might associate the two names, they would not think there was a trade association.	A misrepresentation must be effective: as the public did not think there was a trade association, there was no passing-off. Obiter: if there had been a misrepresentation, the loss of exclusivity in the name might have amounted to actionable damage to reputation.
Edmund Irvine, Tidswell Ltd v Talksport Ltd [2002] EWHC 367, [2002] FSR 60	The defendants used an edited photograph of a racing driver listening to a transistor radio carrying the name of their service as an advertisement. The court found that this was a misrepresentation that Irvine had entered into an endorsement contract with the defendants, and that this damaged the goodwill in his existing product-endorsement business by reducing the opportunities in the broadcasting field.	Businesses in the nature of celebrity endorsement have a protectable goodwill and can prevent unauthorized use of the celebrity image in advertising and activities provided the other elements of the tort are made out.
Chocosuisse Union des Fabricants Suisses de Chocolat v Cadbury Ltd [1999] RPC 826 (CA)	The defendants made (not in Switzerland) 'Swiss Chalet' chocolate. Swiss chocolate manufacturers sued in passing-off. The precise quality attributes of the products of the claimants were somewhat variable, but most products sold as Swiss chocolate had most of the main characteristics.	The *Bollinger* test was made out, despite the variance in the claimant's products.
Ralf Sieckmann v Deutsches Patent-und Markenamt (C-273/00) [2003] RPC 38	S applied to register an olfactory mark for business services by describing it as 'balsamically fruity with a slight hint of cinnamon', giving the name and formula of the chemical that produces the smell and providing a sample.	None of the methods used by S, either individually or collectively, amounted to an adequate graphical representation of the mark for the purposes of **Art 2** of the Directive.
Windsurfing Chiemsee (C-108/97) [1999] ETMR 585	Chiemsee is a lake in Germany. The claimants applied for the mark 'Windsurfing Chiemsee' and were able to demonstrate that the mark had become distinctive of their clothing through use by showing sales and advertising material.	The mark fell within **Art 3(1) (c)**, as it could be used by any clothing company located in the area to describe its goods, so was descriptive. As C had shown acquired distinctiveness, the registration should be allowed.

Key cases

✳✳✳✳✳✳✳✳✳✳

Case	Facts	Principle
SA Societe LTJ Diffusion v Sadas Vertbaudet SA (C-291/00) [2003] ETMR 83	The claimant's mark was 'Arthur'; the defendants used the sign 'Arthur et Felice'. C alleged infringement of trade mark by D inter alia on the ground of an identical mark and goods.	The defendants' sign is identical if it 'reproduces, without any modification or addition, all the elements constituting the trade mark or where, viewed as a whole, it contains differences so insignificant that they may go unnoticed by an average consumer'.
Sabel BV v Puma AG (C-251/95) [1998] RPC 199	Puma had a registered mark of an image of a 'bounding feline'. Sabel applied to register a different image of a bounding feline for the same goods. In S's image, the arrangement of the legs and tail of the cat were different from P's mark.	There must be a likelihood of actual confusion as to the trade origin of the goods to satisfy the confusion test in **Art 4(1)(b)** of the Directive. The possibility of a 'perceived association' is not sufficient.
Intel Corp Inc v CPM United Kingdom Ltd (C-252/07) [2009] RPC 15	Intel's mark 'intel' for items of computer equipment enjoyed a massive reputation. The defendant applied for the name 'Intelmark' for 'telemarketing services', which Intel opposed under **Art 4(4)(a)** (unfair advantage or detriment).	To succeed under the 'detriment' limb of the article, proof was required of a change in the economic behaviour of the average consumer for Intel's goods, or a serious likelihood of it, resulting from Intelmark's use.
L'Oreal SA v Bellure NV (C-487/07) [2010] RPC 1	B sold 'smell-alike' perfumes in similar packaging to that of the claimant's high-value products. B provided a comparison chart indicating which of the claimant's products its products smelt like. B's customers knew that the products were not the claimant's.	B's use of similar packaging was not infringement under **Art 5(1)(b)** because there was no confusion. It was infringement under **Art 5(2)** because customers made an association and B obtained an advantage (it could sell the goods at a premium). B's use was without due cause and the advantage was therefore unfair. The comparison lists infringed under **Art 5(1)(a)** as they were 'used in relation to' the perfume, and the limitation in **Art 6** did not apply.

 **Key debate**

Topic	The scope of the additional protection to be given to trade marks over and above the function of indication of origin
Author	Ilanah Simon Fhima
Standpoint	Discusses the development of ideas of the nature of trade marks and brands since Frank Schechter's 1927 *Harvard Law Review* article, *'The Rational Basis of Trademark Protection'. Points out problems with all the theoretical approaches that have been adopted.*
Source	'Dilution by Blurring—A Conceptual Roadmap' (2010) 1 IPQ 44–87

 **Exam questions**

Problem question

Nigel runs an online children's clothing company called fairydesigns.com. One of his popular lines is a range of knitted sweaters with pictures of animals on them and the name of the animal underneath, for example a picture of an otter with the word 'otter'. Nigel has received a letter from Otterburn Clothing Plc, which runs a chain of outdoor clothing shops called 'Otterburn' and which sell clothing with the brand name 'Otterburn' on their labels. Otterburn Clothing have registered the word OTTERBURN as a trade mark for 'clothing' at the UK Intellectual Property Office. They accuse Nigel of infringing their trade mark and of passing-off. Otterburn also has a logo that appears with the word; this consists of a view of a mountainous skyline (Otterburn is a town in Northumbria, England).

Is Nigel infringing any of Otterburn Clothing's rights and can he challenge its trade mark registration?

See the Outline Answers section in the end matter for help with this question.

Essay question

Critically evaluate the protection given to registered trade marks under **s 10(3)** of the **Trade Marks Act 1994**.

 **Online Resource Centre**

To see an outline answer to this question visit www.oup.com/lawrevision/

Exam essentials

Know what you are aiming at

Intellectual property (IP) examinations may vary between courses more than do examinations in the core subjects:

- There are more issues in IP than can fit into a 20- or 30-credit module. Courses may go for breadth of coverage, or focus on a detailed investigation of a few topics.
- The style of exam and exam question may vary. Questions may be devoted to a single right or require an analysis that includes all potential rights.
- Some examiners pose very brief problems; others present a complex story, where the detailed facts must be analysed for their relevance.
- Essay questions may be focused on a particular area of academic debate that you studied, or may require a discussion of the black-letter law and its application, which draws mainly on primary legal materials.

Your exam may include just one type of question or a mixture of types, and will obviously be focused on what was covered in your course. The balance between problem and essay questions, and the degree of choice, may vary. Ask your tutor about what to expect, and make use of any past papers that are available. The content of your lessons will indicate the breadth and depth of knowledge and application that is required of you.

It is never too early to find out what is expected of you. Some examiners expect a discussion of underlying theoretical and academic debates when answering problem questions, whereas others expect analysis of just the black-letter law, reserving theoretical debate for essay questions. If in doubt, ask.

Answering problem questions
Overall approach

A good approach to solving problems is to read through once to identify potential issues and potential alternative interpretations of the facts, but without getting involved in a detailed analysis. Then go through again making sure that you consider every possible issue and interpretation of the facts you identified first time round. The danger of going straight into a detailed analysis is that by the time you finish it, you will have forgotten that there were other issues to address.

Exam essentials

✱✱✱✱✱✱✱✱✱✱

Things to look for

IP rights (or the possibility of applying for them) arise at a particular stage of a story as a result of what people have done. The story may be expressed, or you may need to construct it.

- Is a business involved and has it started trading?
- Acts of creation are particularly important in giving rise to potential IP rights. Flag up each possible right as it arises.
- Who is the potential owner of the right, and are there any complications (contracts, co-creators, employment)?
- Are there any problems with the right (eg lack of distinctiveness, originality, or inventive step)?
- Do subsequent events prejudice the right (prior disclosures, loss of distinctiveness, the grant of permissions)?

Similarly, with issues of infringement, infringing articles or digital copies are made or created at a particular time and then get passed between people and places. Identify or construct the history from the beginning (manufacture or creation):

- Who is doing each thing—do they have permission, and for what? It may be that you do not know (as in the case of dodgy articles appearing on the market), in which case consider alternatives. Were the products made in the UK or imported; are they genuine or fake? If there is an international element to the activity, free movement of goods principles must be considered.
- What are they doing—is it a potentially infringing act and, if so, which one? Ideally, in your answer you should describe the infringing act (eg 'importing' or 'selling') and also give a statutory reference.
- Where are they doing it? Only UK acts infringe UK law, other acts may infringe local law, which can be addressed with the help of a local lawyer. International conventions and the harmonizing effect of EU law are relevant here.
- Why are they doing it? This may be relevant to the question of whether a defence applies.

Answering essay questions

The broad topics should be clear to you from your course content, though the precise nature of the question might not be. There is no real substitute for reading the underlying materials (textbooks and academic articles, cases) to prepare fully.

You should describe both (or all) sides of an academic debate. Often differences of view stem from different standpoints:

- a purely economics-driven approach will often result in a conclusion that existing legal protection is too extensive (eg copyright duration);

- by starting from a consideration of the rights of a creator/inventor/brand owner a conclusion that more intellectual property is a good thing will often result.

Always be alert to what theoretical standpoint the writer is starting from, and consider what they are ignoring. What about the consumer, or broader social values such as free speech? Conversely, in a market economy, business must be able to make a profit and IP protection is important for that. Having described the debate, you can make your own contribution. Can the conflicting views be explained? Is one view just wrong (and why)? Is there an alternative solution to the problem?

If the essay is more about analysing the black-letter law, this may need analysing from a doctrinal and practical standpoint, as well as in terms of theory and policy. With IP law, the increasing importance of the EU, both in terms of the effect of ECJ case-law on doctrine and the growing importance of the EU in policy-making, must be considered. When considering the practical effects of the law, an appreciation of the facts of the cases, as well as the doctrine developed, is important, as only then can the practical outcome for individuals and businesses be critically discussed.

Revision strategy

Your revision programme should balance learning facts with learning how to answer questions. Practise answering questions of the type you will have to face and try to get feedback on your answers—if not from your tutor, from a fellow student. Lists of what legal issues are relevant to common exam scenarios are useful. This involves organizing information in a different way from the legal headings used in this book. Here are some examples. There are many more:

- the import of goods from inside and outside the EU, where the goods are genuine and where they are fake, for each type of IP right;

- the possibilities for IP protection in relation to surface decoration of a product;

- ways to deal with ex-employees who have taken information (possibly documents) with them;

- circumstances in which freedom of expression and other human rights have an impact on IP law.

Conclusion

How well you do in an exam is mainly down to your ability and how much work you do. But how effective your preparation was also has an effect in helping you to make the most of what you know.

Outline answers

Chapter 2

Problem answer

Various copyright works arise here, but the ones that are relevant to the question are copyright in Kevin's photograph and in the advertisement film. They are the works that have been copied by Kevin and the *Sunday Globe*.

Kevin's photograph will be an artistic work (CDPA, s 4, defines a photograph as a type of artistic work). It thus must be original (s 1(a)). It meets this requirement, as there is nothing to suggest that Kevin copied anything in creating it, and he exercised skill and labour (or intellectual creativity) in doing so (therefore both the traditional UK test and the EU test that may apply as a result of the *Infopaq* decision are met). (The fact that he is well regarded in his field does not affect this, as the test does not require artistic merit.) Kevin will own the copyright as he is the author ('person who creates it'). Kevin is a qualifying person, presumably a UK citizen.

Copyright in a photograph can be infringed by recreating the scene and recording that in some way as the advertising company have done. The question is, have they taken a substantial part of the work (UK test) or a part of the work (EU test)? This means that the part they have taken must be Kevin's original creation (EU test—*Infopaq*), as explained in more recent cases such as *SAS*. In either case, the problem is that only the idea of the scene appears to be taken. This might not amount to a substantial part bearing in mind that the ECJ has embraced the 'idea–expression dichotomy' in *SAS* (though we await a case outside the software field). Thus, we need to know how much detail beyond the idea for the scene has been taken. (A discussion of the legal basis for the 'idea–expression dichotomy' in UK law and of how EU law might view such cases would be appropriate at this point.) Subject to this, copyright has been infringed by making the ad (copying), further acts of copying, and by broadcasting it. The *Sunday Globe* has clearly infringed copyright by reproducing the whole of the work.

The film is also a copyright work, but films do not have to be original, so copyright will exist in it and belong to the producer and principal director—probably the advertising agency will have arranged to own the copyright in their contracts for the production. The CDPA states in s 17(4) that copyright in a film is infringed by copying a single still, so Kevin has infringed in his blog; there is no need to discuss the substantial part test.

It is possible that defences will exist. Kevin can claim that his reproduction of the still was for the purposes of criticism or review of the film, as an accusation of copying relates to the originality (or lack of it) in the film's production, so he is criticizing the film's content (*Time-Warner*). He can also claim the quotation defence. The *Sunday Globe* can claim that the dispute is a current event and they are copying the photograph for the purposes of reporting it. They could also claim criticism and review if the article discusses the artistic aspects of the works and the quotation defence. In both cases, the use must amount to 'fair dealing'—the amount taken must be no more than necessary to report or criticize, or for the purposes of the quote. This appears strongly arguable, as the dispute is closely linked to the exact details of the works and would be difficult to report in words alone.

Chapter 3

Problem answer

Gary will probably have created literary works in his impressions of the games. His database meets the requirements of the definition of a database in the CDPA, s 3A and the Copyright and Rights in Databases Regulations, as it is a collection of works and data which can be separately accessed, so potentially copyright and database right will exist in it.

For copyright to exist, the database must be original in the sense of representing Gary's intellectual creation in the selection and arrangement of its contents. Gary's apparently idiosyncratic choice of which types of match information to record can be said to be creative, so copyright protection may exist. It will potentially protect against someone else copying Gary's choice of categories of match data to use in a different football database. Gary appears to be a qualifying person. The *Football League v Sportradar* case can be distinguished, as there the actual match data were sought to be protected as a selection of information, and copyright in the structure of the database was not asserted.

For database right to exist there must have been substantial investment in the obtaining, verification, or presentation of the data. But according to the *BHB* case, investment in the creation of data, and investment in presenting or verifying it that cannot be separated from the creation of it, does not count. Gary's investment related to his impressions, which are his created data, and would not therefore count, but he is also gathering data (from the pie stalls and by listening to the announcements) and that investment (in his time and effort in recording and so on) would count.

We know from the *Football Dataco v Sportradar* case that a database such as matchinfo.com will not be entitled to copyright protection. However, it clearly satisfies the definition of a database, and there has been substantial investment in making it—the question is, was that investment of the right type (not in creating the data, but in obtaining, verifying, or presenting it)? The match data is free for anyone to collect if they attend the game, so the League is not creator of the data (similarly to Gary's pie data). Thus, there will be database right, since investment in manpower and technology is required and will be substantial (even perhaps for a single match).

Gary takes items of data from it. From the *BHB* case we know that if snippets of data are taken over time and collected together in a database, then the substantial part test is applied to the sum of the bits taken under the 'repeated and systematic' ground in reg 16(2). Over time, therefore, Gary is likely to have taken a substantial part of the database and will therefore be infringing the League's database right. This right will certainly apply to all match data that is not more than 15 years old.

Chapter 4

Problem answer

Mike does not have control over the economic rights in Janice's works, but the moral rights will persist for as long as the copyright (CDPA, s 86(1)). The right to enforce the moral rights will pass with Janice's estate, and this may mean that Mike would be able to enforce them—the details of Janice's will would need to be checked (CDPA, s 96).

First, moral rights depend on copyright, so copyright needs to be established. Janice's lyrics are a literary work and there is nothing to indicate that she was not a qualifying person, so copyright and moral rights exist in them.

The right to object to a derogatory treatment of the work and the right to be attributed as author are both engaged here as the lyrics have been changed, and we are not told that Janice is mentioned on Geraldine's video.

For there to be derogatory treatment there must be a treatment of the work. There is, as the lyrics have been modified (their internal structure has been changed). To be derogatory, the treatment must be prejudicial to Janice's honour or reputation (it does not have to amount to a distortion or mutilation)—s 80(2)(b).

There is a dearth of case law to tell us what is a derogatory treatment, but the facts here do go beyond those cases saying what it is not such as *Pasterfield* and *Confetti Records*. Mike should produce evidence of Janice's artistic reputation and how she was viewed by her public (required according to *Confetti*) and argue that a consistent political standpoint is part of an artist's honour and reputation that should be protected.

For there to be actual infringement of Janice's moral rights, Geraldine must have done one of the acts the CDPA prescribes in relation to Janice's work. Placing on the internet amounts to 'communicating to the public' under CDPA, s 80(3)(a) and so there is infringement. However, in the case of song lyrics, it is not an act that requires an attribution as author; therefore only the one moral right can be infringed by Geraldine. Also, we do not know if Janice ever asserted her right to be acknowledged as author (although this is likely, as she was a professional).

Outline answers

✱✱✱✱✱✱✱✱✱✱

Geraldine is infringing, but if yourvid.com are notified they will become infringers and can be asked to take the video down from their site.

Chapter 5

Problem answer

Each band member will have a performer's right in their performance as a musical performance (CDPA, s 180(2)) (*Experience Hendrix*). A right will arise each time they perform on stage. Their performances will qualify for protection as they are UK nationals, so we do not need to enquire if Russia is a qualifying country for the purposes of performers' rights. Subject to any agreement between the band members about enforcing their rights, or any recording contract they may have, Chopper can enforce his performer's rights regardless of what the others think.

The act of recording the performance took place in Russia so is not an infringement under the CDPA (it is possibly an infringement of Russian law). We do not know where the DVDs were copied, but this was probably also not in the UK (maybe in Portugal). So although recording a performance and making copies are infringements of the performers' property rights under the CDPA, ss 182 and 182A, the Act will not help us in this case. Similarly, the act of issuing copies (placing the copies on the market for the first time—s 182B) probably happened in Portugal (the dealer), not the UK. However, as this aspect of the law is harmonized EU-wide in the Rental Rights Directive, we can be reasonably confident that with the help of a Portuguese lawyer we might be able to sue the dealer for issuing copies to the public and possibly making the copies.

The acts which took place in the UK are importing and selling copies, by Sideways Records. These are infringing acts, but in each case there is a knowledge requirement similar to secondary infringing acts in relation to copyright (s 184). Did Sideways know or have reason to believe the recordings were illicit (made without the performers' consent—s 197)? If the documentary appears professional, they might reasonably assume that the necessary consents were obtained, so they will have this defence.

Chopper can inform the shop that the recordings are indeed illicit, but the shop will have the defence of 'innocent acquisition' (s 184(2)), meaning that they will only be liable to pay a reasonable sum in relation to their existing stock, though they will not be able to purchase and sell further copies. (Note: if the DVDs came from outside the EU such that Sideways were issuers, they would have no such defences.)

Chapter 6

Problem answer

Henry has recognized a business opportunity and not told his employer about it. Arguably, this is a breach of his duty of faithful service to his employer, though this would depend on the precise nature of his duties as a salesman. If his duties as a salesman included the duty to promote the interests of Educational by identifying market information and feeding it back to them, this could place him under a fiduciary duty, as in *Helmet Integrated Systems*. This would mean that (notwithstanding that he had the idea in his spare time) he was under a duty to reveal it to Educational, and the idea is their information in equity.

The result of this is that Henry would be in breach of his duties by exploiting his idea (which is in fact Educational's trade secret) and revealing it to Stylish. However, as Stylish now have the idea, it may be impossible to obtain an injunction to restrain them from using it if they obtained it in good faith, even if Educational now notify them that it is their idea. It is in the public domain by being used in schools (*Spycatcher*). Educational could obtain damages from Henry (*Seager v Copydex*), but not Stylish if they acted in good faith.

In addition, Henry appears to be making use of his customer contact information to sell the new product and others in competition with Educational. The bare list of contacts is confidential but easily gathered from the public domain (lists of schools and so on). If Henry took the information away in his head, following *Faccenda* there is nothing Educational can do about it as it forms part of Henry's skill and knowledge in his job. If he took a printed or electronic list with him, that could be a breach of confidence, but as the information is public, an injunction restraining Henry would only be granted for a limited time. As this information is so easy to obtain, possibly no injunction would be considered proportionate (*Vestergaard*) to Henry's breach. Henry may be making use of further information about individual customers that is not public and would have to be gathered over time, and if this is the case the information may be protectable for a period.

In relation to the customer information, Stylish would be potentially liable for its use, as they should have realized that Henry was making use of Educational's secret information (distinguish *Thomas v Pearce*). Educational should contact them about this, as they may agree to restrain Henry's activities once their legal obligations are made clear to them.

As it appears that Henry has left unilaterally, Educational may be able to insist that he works out his notice period by staying at home ('garden leave'), enabling his successor salesperson to establish a relationship with customers. We should also check if there are any restrictive covenants in Henry's contract, though we are not told that there are any.

Chapter 7

Problem answer

Peter has identified that a particular chemical substance (parsnipin) has an effect in repelling rodents. This satisfies the main requirements for patentability apart from novelty and obviousness: it is a development in a technical field and is capable of industrial application (by making and selling the chemical)—PA 1977, s 1.

There are a number of novelty issues, however. An invention is not new if it has been made available to the public (s 2(2)). First, parsnipin is known as a food additive. This is not a problem, as Peter is proposing a different use for the product (putting in an attic to repel squirrels, not putting in food). So there is novelty of use.

Secondly, the general class of chemicals to which parsnipin belongs is known to repel rodents. However, parsnipin appears to work better than members of the class generally,

indicating that a different technical effect is at work. Novelty can be established in these circumstances under the principles governing 'selection patents' (*Bayer, Dr Reddys*).

Thirdly, some information about the invention has been disclosed to Dave and Jane. The question here is whether that was an enabling disclosure. Peter will want to patent parsnipin, as this is likely to be commercially useful, rather than use of a bag of dry parsnips, and he has not disclosed parsnipin, so these disclosures do not make an invention claiming parsnipin available to the public. It might be possible to argue that the disclosures to them were in confidence, although the facts given do not really suggest this—this point needs investigating.

So, the invention should not fail for lack of novelty on the basis of the facts given, although further searches that the patent office will carry out may reveal prior art, which does disclose the invention.

As for obviousness, this would be a matter for expert evidence. If Peter's own disclosure is not in the prior art, the prospects are not bad. Would it be obvious to try all members of the rodexin family (or are there too many of them for this)? If Peter's disclosures are in the prior art, then the arguments for obviousness building on that are stronger. If a 'problem-and-solution' approach is taken, would it have been obvious to investigate known rodent repellents and the chemical make-up of parsnips as Peter did? The UK *Pozzoli* approach would lead to a similar question of fact for the expert witnesses in this situation.

Chapter 8

Problem answer

Sarah has created products (furniture) with an appearance, so she may be able to apply for a registered design and have the EU unregistered right (RDA, s 1). She has created articles with shape and configuration, so UK unregistered design right might apply (CDPA, s 213(1)–(3)). Her carvings may amount to sculptures or works of artistic craftsmanship, so copyright may exist under CDPA, s 4.

Applying *Lucasfilm*, the question of copyright in Sarah's carvings as sculptures depends on her intention and all the circumstances of the

Outline answers

✱✱✱✱✱✱✱✱✱✱

case. Were the carvings intended primarily to be admired for their appearance, or was the main purpose functional? Probably if the main intention was to sit on/at them, the definition is not met. But assuming there was an aesthetic element to her work and that it is individually crafted, the furniture items are probably works of artistic craftsmanship.

Domen may argue that they are entitled to the s 51 defence, that the furniture shapes are designs but are not 'designs for artistic works'. Clearly, carved furniture items are 'designs' as they involve shape and appearance and not surface decoration. Whether they are 'designs for' artistic works probably depends on Sarah's intention when creating them (*Lucasfilm* in the Court of Appeal), rather than an objective assessment. Sarah did not appear to have any intention to create designs for mass production, so if her furniture has copyright protection the s 51 defence will not apply.

There appears to be copying based on the detailed features that are reproduced, so the chairs are infringing articles. Assuming they are made in the Netherlands, the infringing acts committed in the UK will be importing into the UK, keeping and selling by the garden centre—secondary infringing acts under CDPA, ss 22 and 23. The garden centre will not infringe if they lack knowledge (they have no means of knowing that the furniture is infringing), so they must be put on notice. The garden centre is not an issuer as it appears Domen placed the items on the EU market, so the primary infringing act of issuing under s 18 is not relevant here.

UK design right will apply subject to the test for originality. If the designs are commonplace in the design field in question (s 213(4)), they will not be original for the purposes of design right. This type of furniture is known, but research into the design field is needed. If the right exists, it is infringed by the garden centre as with copyright, though there is additionally a defence of innocent acquisition that may be available.

The EU unregistered right under Art 19(2) of the Regulation may apply if the furniture has an appearance that is new and has individual character. 'Appearance' for this purpose will include the texture of the surfaces, for example the wood grain and chainsaw marks.

Novelty is worldwide, though only designs known to the trade in the EU count. Individual character requires a different overall impression on the informed user (who will be a furniture purchaser who takes care to investigate the market—*Grupo Promer*). This will also require investigation. Subject to this, the EU unregistered right is an anti-copying right, so it may have been infringed. As it is an EU-wide right, it may be worth instructing a Dutch lawyer to assert it against Domen, as well as asserting it in the UK against the garden centre. However, this right only lasts for three years from the first marketing of articles (which would be the tearoom display).

Sarah should consider applying for a registered design for her furniture; the tests for novelty and distinctive character are as set out earlier. The advantage would be that this gives a monopoly right. However, Sarah must apply within 12 months of the display of the furniture in the tearooms, otherwise that will count as prior art, removing novelty.

Chapter 9

Problem answer

First, for passing-off Otterburn must show that they have goodwill that is associated in the minds of the pubic with their name, 'Otterburn'. This is clearly the case. Next, they must show that Nigel's use of the name 'Otter' and/or the picture of an otter amounts to a misrepresentation that his products are made by Otterburn or associated with them in some way, for example by licensing. This is a question of fact. But as the words are not very similar (and the logos are different) Otterburn will probably have to produce evidence of confusion among customers, for example misdirected complaints or compliments, etc. Not all customers need to be confused, only a significant proportion (*Taittinger v Allbev*).

As for trade mark infringement, following *Arsenal* Nigel will be using the word 'otter' and the image 'in relation to' clothing, so the question will hinge on confusion. Nigel is not using a mark that is identical to OTTERBURN but he is using one part of the compound word. The otter image, by conveying the concept of an otter, is also potentially infringing. Nigel is using his signs on the same goods as those for which OTTERBURN is registered (clothing). The test for ordinary infringement under s 10(2) as interpreted by the ECJ in *Sabel* is thus whether consumers for this type of product will think there is a trade association between fairydesigns.com and Otterburn Clothing as a result of the similarity between the marks and the fact that they are used on identical goods. All the circumstances of the case, including how well known the mark OTTERBURN is, are taken into account.

Otterburn could also try to argue that Nigel's use of a similar mark is 'without due cause' and takes unfair advantage of, or is detrimental to, the character or repute of their mark under the TMA, s 10(3). The facts do not indicate any advantage and Nigel can argue that

the mainly decorative nature of his use is due cause. For there to be detriment, there would have to be an effect on the behaviour of consumers in relation to Otterburn's goods as a result of Nigel's use (*Intel*). Success under this heading for Otterburn seems unlikely.

As Otterburn is a place, there is a potential challenge to the trade mark registration on the basis that the registration should not have been granted (TMA, s 47(1)). However, this objection can be overcome by distinctiveness acquired by use of the mark and, in the case of a challenge to a registered mark, that use can be made since the mark was registered. Given Otterburn's trading, they have presumably acquired distinctiveness, and this will overcome any objection on this ground (*Windsurfing*).

Glossary

Attribution One of the moral rights of authors is the right to be attributed as author of their work. Another is the right not to be falsely attributed as the author of a work.

Authorial works Works that require originality for protection, different from entrepreneurial works.

Authors' rights Copyright in the works that require originality and moral rights are collectively known as 'authors' rights'.

Claim(s) A series of numbered paragraphs in a patent, each of which describes in words an invention. Only things that fall within the scope of a claim can infringe the patent.

Computer program(s) The protection of programs by copyright is harmonized by an EU Directive. Programs may also be protected by patents, provided they involve a development in technology beyond pure computer programming.

Configuration This is a concept relevant to UK design right and copyright protection for designs. It is related to shape, but may also include elements of connectedness and organization.

Confusion A requirement for both passing-off and trade mark infringement where either the two marks or the goods they are used on are not identical.

Database(s) There is an EU Directive that defines databases and sets out how copyright law must protect (or not protect) them and also sets up a separate sui generis right in the contents of a database.

Derogatory treatment There is a moral right to object to derogatory treatment of a work.

Descriptiveness Trade marks that are descriptive of the goods or services for which they are applied may be refused unless it can be shown that they have acquired distinctiveness.

Distinctiveness Trade marks cannot be registered unless they are distinctive of the goods or services of the applicant for which the trade mark is applied for.

Entrepreneurial works See 'Neighbouring rights'.

Free movement of goods An important concept of EU law that overrides intellectual property rights in goods once they have been placed on the EU market by or with the consent of the rights owner.

Goods and services When applying for a registered trade mark, the applicant must specify the goods or services for which registration is sought and must be using or intend to use the mark on those goods.

Goodwill The tort of passing-off is based on the notion of a misrepresentation that causes loss to the goodwill of a business; therefore goodwill in a business is a necessary element of passing-off.

Individual character A requirement for a design to be registered: even if the design is new it must also have individual character; that is, give a different overall impression to the informed user of the product.

Industrial application This is another requirement for an invention to be patented: discoveries and theories lack this so cannot be patented, although a practical application can.

Intellectual creation The test for originality used in EU legislation and now part of UK law, although it is not clear that it is different from the skill and labour test.

Joint tortfeasorship A general principle of tort law that means someone can be liable for procuring or assisting a wrong by another—increasingly important in dealing with internet businesses that assist infringing activities.

Neighbouring rights Rights related to copyright or (in the UK) considered part of copyright but which do not require originality: sound recordings, fixations of films, published editions, and broadcasts (see 'Entrepreneurial works'); and performers' rights.

Novelty Patents and registered designs cannot be registered unless they are new.

Obviousness Another requirement for patentability is that even if an invention is new it cannot be patented if it was an obvious development at the time.

Olfactory marks Such as smells and tastes cannot be registered as trade marks.

Originality A requirement for protection of some works as defined in Art 2 of the **Berne Convention** and as 'literary, dramatic, musical or artistic works' by the **Copyright, Designs and Patents Act 1988**. It means that the work must come from the author and have involved either skill and labour or intellectual creation.

Owner The first owner of the statutory property IP rights is defined in the statute. Subsequently, ownership can be transferred. Moral rights and performers' rights are personal to authors and performers, so do not have owners.

Primary infringement Acts which infringe copyright where no knowledge of the infringing nature of the activity is required.

Prior art All those things made available to the public before the priority date of a patent which, if they disclose the invention claimed, will mean it is not new and cannot be patented.

Secondary infringement Acts that infringe copyright only if the infringer has knowledge of the infringing nature of the activity, for example knowledge that a product is an unlawful copy of a work.

Shape Trade marks can be registered that consist of the shape of goods or their packaging, though specific exclusions apply. In addition, shapes can be protected by registered designs, unregistered design rights, and copyright. If a shape results in a technical effect, it can be patented.

Skill and labour The traditional UK test for originality; it has been replaced by the 'intellectual creation' test.

Specification A patent specification consists of claims and a description. The claims are interpreted in light of the specification as a whole.

Substantial investment A requirement for a database to be protected by the sui generis right.

Surface decoration Protectable by copyright, a registered design, and the EU unregistered right, but not by UK design right.

Teaching A patent specification must teach the skilled person how to put the invention claimed into effect, otherwise the patent is invalid.

Technical character Only inventions that have technical character can be patented; it is a fundamental principle of European patent law.

Work(s) A generic term for things protected by copyright. In the UK, this includes neighbouring rights (apart from performers' rights); in many other countries they are not regarded as works.

Index

Index

✳✳✳✳✳✳✳✳✳✳✳✳

Index

✳✳✳✳✳✳✳✳✳✳

Index

****

Index